Lost and Found

LOST AND FOUND

*Historic and Natural Landmarks
of the San Gabriel Valley*

*For Mary Murphy,
best wishes!*

E LIZABETH   P OMEROY

*at the Los Angeles Times Festival of Books,
April 2003.*

Elizabeth Pomeroy

MANY
MOONS
PRESS

Lost and Found: Historic and Natural Landmarks of the San Gabriel Valley, First Edition, was produced by Regina Books and printed by Cushing-Malloy, Inc..

Second Printing, 2001

Book design is by Mark Morrall Dodge.

The watercolor painting on the cover, showing the Colorado Street Bridge and Vista del Arroyo, is by Joseph Stoddard. He also provided the pen and ink sketches done on location for the section divider pages.

Cover design and art direction are by Hortensia Chu. She also created the Many Moons Press logo.

ISBN 0-9700481-0-6

MANY
MOONS
PRESS

P.O. Box 94505
Pasadena, California 91109

PRINTED IN THE UNITED STATES OF AMERICA

Contents

NORTH

Preface

This is a book of stories, and it is also a guide to historic places. I hope you will enjoy the reading and then the discoveries you will make out "in the field." Some of these are preservation success stories; may they inspire you to see opportunities nearby.

These articles are selected from five years of my weekly newspaper column "Lost and Found". They all originally appeared in the *San Gabriel Valley Tribune*, the *Pasadena Star-News*, and the *Whittier Daily News*. The series is continuing.

I am grateful to many curators, docents, and others who gladly show visitors these historic resources. Thanks in particular to Sue Mossman (Pasadena Heritage), Tania Rizzo (Pasadena Historical Museum Archives), Fred Love (El Monte Historical Museum), and Denzil Heaney (Whittier Historical Museum) for sharing their photographs, files, and knowledge. Every story here has helpful people behind it, who know the history and where to find things in their crowded archives.

Special thanks to Cathie Lou Parker, the editor with the San Gabriel Valley Newspapers who first signed me on to write the column. Richard D. Burns and Mark Dodge did the skilled production work for this book. The cover designer and artistic "presiding spirit" was Hortensia Chu. Joseph Stoddard created five original drawings especially for the book. That's his traveling paint box on the back cover.

And thanks to readers (some even from out of state) who have written to me with topics, childhood memories, or that irresistible question: "Is it still there?" I had to go and find out.

If time is the fourth dimension, then your knowledge of the past will add a new dimension to your enjoyment of these surroundings, even the places familiar from every day.

I would like to hear from you. Thanks for joining me.

Elizabeth Pomeroy
Pasadena, California
January 2000

How to Enjoy your Lost and Found Adventures

These historic vignettes are arranged in four groups: North, South, East and West, to make it easier for you to visit several places in one day. Within these groups, the cities are arranged alphabetically. The area covered is the San Gabriel Valley and just beyond, with sites from Pasadena to Whittier, Tujunga to Rancho Cucamonga: over 100 historic places in 40 cities.

* Directions given in this book begin from the freeway nearest to the site. You will need your local street map or Thomas Guide as a reference also.

* Call a site before you visit, especially if you'll be travelling a distance. Many historic places are kept going by dedicated volunteers. The open hours may change, or the place may be closed for renovation.

* When you have time, take the streets, not the freeways, to these historic spots. You'll see the geography and the surroundings of the landmark so much better. Even a mighty river like the San Gabriel River goes almost unnoticed if you cross it among trucks at freeway speed. If you cross it on a city street, you might see that white egret among the reeds.

* Walking is better yet. Take a walk around the neighborhood of the historic site. You'll see all of that little stone church from more of a distance, and you can imagine its original setting.

* Take your camera or sketch pad. When you're composing a picture, you'll notice things you might otherwise have missed.

* Have you visited the oldest cemetery in your town? Take your time and look and read. If you first review your local history, the names will be familiar.

* Often, individuals in town have memories of the early days. You can find out who they are and maybe meet them. Perhaps you could help gather oral histories.

* Leave a contribution; buy a memento. Your support will keep the Lost and Found treasure available to future generations.

* Your time is a valuable gift too. Volunteer hours are fun and they will put you in the heart of history.

* See if your town has an archive or library of its history. This may be in the public library, a local historical society, or even in city hall. You might call the chamber of commerce for ideas. The keepers of a historic building may have a collection you can consult there. Such materials rarely circulate, so set aside an afternoon to read and look at old photographs.

And now, fellow history-hunters, let's go exploring.

church of the Angels-Pasadena California

Farnsworth Park

✧ *Altadena* ✧

To TRACE THE social history of a town, look at the activities in one of its favorite parks over the years. This method works beautifully with Altadena's 15-acre General Charles S. Farnsworth County Park.

The sloping tract of foothill land, high at the top of Lake Avenue, was a simple homestead until 1916, when the Los Angeles County Forestry Department established a tree nursery there. Incense cedar and Coulter pine seedlings flourished, but the operation was moved to Henninger Flat (along the Mt. Wilson Toll Road) in 1929 for better growing conditions.

Retired World War I Army General Farnsworth persuaded County officials to develop the land as a public park. A Board of Control, with representatives from 23 Altadena community groups, would oversee operations. A handsome recreation building was completed in October 1934 and named for William D. Davies, an organizer of the project.

The Depression was at hand, and the Davies Memorial Building was constructed by the Works Progress Administration (WPA) to give work to Altadena's unemployed. (More than 165 WPA projects still survive in Southern California). The steel and concrete building is said to be California's first public structure made earthquake resistant. The rustic, lodge-like building is made of wood shingles and cobblestones hauled by mule from the Arroyo Seco. Inside are a lower and an upper auditorium, storage, kitchens, and banquet rooms. The total cost was $50,187. An outdoor amphitheater south of the building seats 800 for summer plays and other amusements.

The official dedication in June 1939 featured horseshoe tournaments, tennis, and soft-ball; also music by the Pasadena Federal Chamber Symphony. Speakers praised the land developed from a wild poppyfield into a place dedicated "to human betterment." 715 people played and picnicked on opening day.

In 1945 a town notice announced the Annual Altadena Country Fair. Entry blanks at all schools urged students to "show your best chickens, rabbits, vegetables." There would be "trophies galore" for the winners, plus music talent shows and track meets.

Through the '40s and '50s, fiestas were held at the park by Los Fiesteros, a group created to keep alive the fiesta spirit and early traditions of Southern California.

In the 1970s there were Easter Egg Hunts, the summer Shakespeare Festival, a Black History Festival, and cabaret nights, plus sports, community picnics, and play groups. In the '90s a Recycling Fair featured the Recyclones, a young advocacy group. For almost 60 years, the Theatre Americana, billed as the first community theater program in the U.S., performed in the Davies Building.

A history like this is cause for celebration, and so a rededication event was held in summer of 1988. Art workshops and horseshoe matches mixed with aerobics classes for a contemporary note. Today, playing fields and a host of activities for children and teens keep this park very much alive.

How to get there: Farnsworth Park is at the corner of Lake Ave. and Mt. Curve Ave. From the 210 Freeway, exit at Lake Ave. and drive north. Call (626) 798-6335, Monday through Friday.

Cobb Estate

⟡ *Altadena* ⟡

BORDERS BETWEEN TOWNS and wild areas are often fascinating in Southern California. The Cobb Estate in Altadena is one such place, criss-crossed by human activity over many years.

The property lies at the foot of the San Gabriel Mountains, just above Altadena's old poppy fields. At the top of Lake Avenue are stone gates and a winding entrance road, into hilly grounds now going wild. To the east is Las Flores Canyon, a major water source for the early settlers. Just beyond that is the three-mile Sam Merrill Trail to Echo Mountain, where Professor Thaddeus Lowe's white hotel overlooked the valley a hundred years ago.

Ample water and an ocean view attracted Robert Forsyth to this land in the 19th century. He settled on 107 acres. A burst of gold mining followed, when William Twaddell staked out claims a mile into the canyon. In 1893 and 1894, he worked mines called the Golden Star, Jessie Marie, Monitor, and Bald Eagle. A wagon road probed the

canyon. Tunnels as long as 65 feet were cut by dynamite and hand tools into the rock walls.

A processing mill was begun near the canyon mouth. There was gold, but no profit, so the work was soon abandoned and the tunnels sealed.

When Charles J. Cobb of Lincoln, Maine, bought the property in 1916, he found an orange grove, a large reservoir, and an old house still occupied by Twaddell. Cobb had made a fortune as a lumber executive in Seattle, then came to Altadena at age 64. He built a substantial tile-roofed mansion, with Italian cypress and eucalyptus trees along his driveway. His wife Carrie sold their oranges to local markets. Twaddell was welcome to stay put until his death in 1920.

Cobb was a 32nd degree Mason and contributed to the Scottish Rite Cathedral in Pasadena. At his death in 1939, his residence became a Masonic Home. From 1942-55 it was a retreat for the nuns of St. Luke's Hospital. Then plans for a subdivision came and went. The house stood empty, beset by vandals.

The last private owners were Groucho, Harpo, and Gummo Marx, who bought the property in 1960, razed the house, and in 1971 considered selling out to a cemetery association. At this point, John Muir High School students secured a pledge from Pasadena philanthropist Virginia Steele Scott, plus other contributions, to buy the property. The Audubon Society helped transfer the land to the U.S. Forest Service.

Today hikers pass through the Cobb Estate, headed for Echo Mountain and deeper into the range. History buffs will find stone foundations, and reservoirs still belonging to the Las Flores Water Company (formed in 1885). On the slopes below the estate, where shining poppies once could be seen from the ocean, the name of Poppyfields Drive remains.

As you stroll in the Cobb Estate, you'll be in that ever-changing borderland between town and mountains.

How to get there: From the 210 Freeway, exit at Lake Ave. and drive north to its end. Contact the Altadena Historical Society at (626) 794-4961.

St. Elizabeth's Church
✧ *Altadena* ✧

THIS MAY BE the prettiest tower for miles around. But don't just settle for a picture of it. Go and see St. Elizabeth's Church in Altadena on one of these blue-sky days, when the sky shows through the white tower with its hand-made Mexican tiles.

A Roman Catholic congregation first began meeting near here in 1918. They occupied a storage room in a grocery store, mingling incense with the smell of potatoes (according to a parish historian).

But help was at hand. Andrew McNally, a founder of Rand-McNally, had bought some Altadena property in 1887 and lived there in a handsome house which still stands. By the 1920's his grandson, Wallace Neff, was becoming an architect who would typify Southern California's "Golden Age."

Neff was born in La Mirada, California, in 1895 and spent five years in Europe, studying the native buildings of Italy,

Germany, France, England, and Spain. In 1920 he began to practice architecture in Pasadena and stayed throughout his career.

Over his lifetime he designed dozens of houses resembling Spanish mills, Norman farm houses, or English dwellings. Some were for Hollywood stars such as Mary Pickford, Groucho Marx, and Cary Grant. His signature style was the Spanish Colonial Revival—simple architecture of Spain and rural Mexico, with stucco walls, arches, and wrought iron.

In this vein, he created his only church design: St. Elizabeth's. At its dedication in 1926, a local newspaper described it as "medieval Spanish," and "Old World art with New World comfort."

The elegant tower rises 100 feet, decorated with blue and yellow tiles. The southern loggia catches the sun. The church is at an angle to the street, inviting viewers to walk around it. The entrance terrace and steps are wide semi-circles, leading to a deeply sheltered doorway.

If you take your camera, you'll find many angles where the white walls, the architectural forms, the tile roofs, plants and sky make beautiful compositions. This is perhaps the genius of Neff: the pleasure of his buildings from so many angles.

Since you're on foot, don't miss two other surprises. Neff also designed the Shrine of the Little Flower, completed in 1930 just behind the church. The statue of the Virgin Mary has a tiny pool at her feet, a blue mosaic background, and a scallop shell over her niche.

North of the parking lot is the grotto called Lourdes of the West. Ryozo Fuso (Louis) Kado, the fifth generation of a family of rock artists, made this shrine in 1939. It is a cave 25 feet high, formed of 130 tons of lava rock from Mono Lake reinforced by concrete and steel.

Statues and candles rest on natural ledges, while a waterfall cascades into a pool. Nearby is a concrete outdoor pulpit, made to look like a huge tree stump. Tall old deodars keep silence around the shrine.

How to get there: St. Elizabeth's is at 1849 N. Lake Ave. From the 210 Freeway, exit at Lake and drive north. Call (626) 797-1167.

Pacific Electric Substation No. 8

◇ *Altadena* ◇

HISTORY SEEKERS IN Southern California know some familiar silhouettes: the long barn-like buildings that were citrus packing houses, or the eaves of a Craftsman-style dwelling. Now what about that solid, brick building on Lake Avenue in Altadena, obviously old? Its shape says: "railroads."

This is the Pacific Electric Railway Substation No. 8. Its origins go back to Professor Thaddeus Lowe's famed Mount Lowe Railway, which once climbed to Echo Mountain and the Alpine Tavern in the San Gabriel Mountains. This rail line rose a total of 3,130 feet above Altadena in about six miles.

Electric power generating facilities were on Echo Mountain, reached by the first leg of the railway in 1893. Also on this scenic knoll was the Echo Mountain House, a white hotel of 70 bedrooms and sweeping verandas, easily seen from below and known as the "White City."

But fire brought down the hotel in 1900, only six years after it opened. Professor Lowe's fortunes were faltering, and in 1902 the

Pasadena & Mount Lowe Railway was bought by a newcomer to California, Henry Huntington.

The mountain route was added to Huntington's Pacific Electric Railway (the Red Cars), which opened up so much of Southern California. But new generating facilities were needed to replace those lost in the fire. So the Altadena Substation was built in 1906. It contained motor-generators which fed the P.E.'s local line in Pasadena and Altadena, as well as the mountain line.

A few remember today the last journey of the Mount Lowe Railway, in December 1937. With automobiles bringing people into the mountains, the historic line was losing its savor. The Depression struck a blow. And in 1936, the Alpine Tavern, destination of thousands over the years, burned down.

Just three months after that last run, the monumental floods of March 1938 scrubbed away much of the abandoned track and trestles.

In the cities below, traces of the Pacific Electric remained. The Altadena Substation had various business uses. A survivor from a vanished way of transportation, it held on as modern Altadena rose around it.

But in 1977 it faced demolition. Mt. Lowe historian Charles Seims and the Altadena Historical Society succeeded in getting the structure listed on the National Register of Historic Places. A real estate firm undertook earthquake-reinforcing, then used the building as their offices.

Today the substation is very much alive, occupied by a firm of architects which handles, among other things, creative re-uses for old buildings. Inside you can see the wall once covered by breaker panels and meters. Opposite are the outlets which provided power to a multitude of Red Cars and mountain trolleys.

Now that you know this shape, which says "railroads," have you spotted the similar brick building on Fair Oaks Avenue just south of Glenarm in Pasadena?

How to get there: The Altadena Substation is at 2245 N. Lake Ave. From the 210 Freeway, exit at Lake Ave. and drive north. Call the Altadena Historical Society at (626) 794-4961.

Santa Anita Railroad Depot
✧ *Arcadia* ✧

PASSING ON BUSY Baldwin Avenue in Arcadia, opposite the Santa Anita Racetrack, you may see the little train station and ask, "Is that something old, or new?" The answer is, it's both.

In the 1880s, Elias Jackson Baldwin, known as "Lucky," was acquiring San Gabriel Valley lands which finally totaled 46,000 acres. From the homeplace of his Santa Anita Ranch, now the Los Angeles County Arboretum, Baldwin managed 500 acres of orange groves, English walnuts, lemons, peaches, almonds, and other fruits.

Hundreds of sheep, cattle, and hogs flourished, and among his several hundred horses were 70 pampered thoroughbreds bearing Baldwin's red and black racing silks. Historians agree that Baldwin tended to be land rich and cash poor, but he was lucky with the coming of the railroads to Southern California.

Wishing to sell off some of his land, Baldwin contracted with the Los Angeles and San Gabriel Valley Railroad (later part of the Santa Fe) to build its line from Los Angeles across his ranch. The two-

story Gothic-styled Santa Anita Depot was complete in 1890 at a cost of $5,000, using some 100,000 bricks from Baldwin's own brickyard.

The little building, originally a quarter mile north of the Arboretum on Colorado Blvd., served passengers and freight for the ranch and the town of Sierra Madre. Nearby residents picked up mail there. The depot soon hummed with five passenger trains and several freight trains stopping daily. Upstairs were living quarters for the depot agent and family.

But commerce shifted even as the town of Arcadia grew (founded by Baldwin, its first mayor, in 1903). The depot was officially closed in 1940. Boarded up, it stood forgotten until ironic news reached the community in 1962: the little station stood in the path of the proposed Foothill Freeway (the 210).

In a "Save the Depot" effort, the Arcadia Historical Society, Los Angeles County, the Santa Fe Railroad, citizens and schoolchildren all pulled together. The depot was dismantled, moved, and rebuilt within the Arboretum for $32,500, opening once again in 1970.

Step into the waiting room, once a hub of daily activity. The brick fireplace is unusual in train stations, but the sectioned waiting benches are typical fare. Trunks, satchels and hat boxes of old are stacked in a corner. On the wall, a bird's eye view map of Arcadia in 1887 predates the depot by a few years. Note the pictures of Baldwin's three big hotels: in San Francisco, Arcadia, and at Lake Tahoe (all now gone).

Visit the adjacent kitchen and agent's office, both furnished with turn-of-the-century necessities: a telegraph set, a 1904 adding machine, an early "copier," and more photographs.

Upstairs are a snug parlor and bedroom. Nora Higginson, depot agent 1895-98, whose photograph is there on her desk, must have enjoyed this domestic retreat.

How to get there: The Arboretum is at 301 N. Baldwin Ave. in Arcadia. From the 210 Freeway, exit at Baldwin and drive south. For information call (626) 821-3222.

Queen Anne Cottage
Los Angeles County Arboretum
◇ *Arcadia* ◇

THE GUEST HOUSE had been vacant for 40 years, its only "tenants" being bats and termites. Windows gone, doors gone—an occasional owl was a guest by day. A gothic tale? No, this was the condition of the Queen Anne Cottage at the Los Angeles County Arboretum, in 1949.

Once this property was the 8,500-acre Rancho Santa Anita, owned by Los Angeles magnate Harris Newmark and his associates. Then came Ohio-born Elias Jackson ("Lucky") Baldwin, that master of venture capitalism. With funds from Nevada silver mining, he bought the ranch in 1875 for $200,000. It was the largest real estate transaction up to that time in Los Angeles.

Under Baldwin, the ranch was amazingly productive. Records showed 500 acres of orange groves, nearly a million young nursery

trees, 3000 English walnut trees, and almost every fruit tree that could flourish in this climate; plus vineyards, experimental tobacco and cotton—it was almost Eden run wild.

After converting an adobe on the property for his own home, Baldwin built a fanciful Queen Anne-style guest house. The little building, finished in 1886, had four rooms and a bath but no kitchen. An artesian well in front sometimes threw water to a height of six feet, providing a little lake.

The *Los Angeles Times* called this miniature house "Baldwin's Belvedere", while California historian H.H. Bancroft called it "a little bijou residence." Some of the furnishings were brought from the Baldwin Hotel in San Francisco. Marble steps, pictorial glasswork, and the bric-a-brac of the day created a little party spot for enjoying the Baldwin wines.

After incorporating the city of Arcadia and becoming its mayor (1903), and opening the first Santa Anita Racetrack (1907), Lucky Baldwin died at his ranch in 1909.

127 acres of that private Eden became the Los Angeles County Arboretum in 1947. But the three historic structures on the land were in sad shape. The first to be restored was the guest house, known thereafter (but not in Baldwin's time) as the Queen Anne Cottage. Among tall trees, it stood somewhere between weathered charm and dangerous dry rot.

Curator Maurice Block of the Huntington Art Gallery guided the interior restoration. Scraping the paint revealed the original white and red colors. "A certain gaiety" was the goal for the house, said Mr. Block, as though guests were expected.

Meanwhile, the contractor worked on repairs for a year and a half. He shored up the tower and removed the bees that had stored 75 pounds of honey there. The restoration was complete in 1954.

Today, the Queen Anne Cottage, with the lake at its feet and the mountains behind, speaks of the fun-loving Baldwin. The Cottage is open only on rare occasions like the Christmas Open House, but visitors may look into the many windows or admire its tower .

How to get there: The Arboretum is at 301 N. Baldwin Ave. in Arcadia. From the 210 Freeway, exit at Baldwin and drive south. For information, call (626) 821-3222.

U.S. Army Balloon School
✧ *Arcadia* ✧

IN 1918, RESIDENTS of Arcadia might have imagined they saw Dumbo and the Flying Elephants overhead. This strange sight in wartime was the 90-foot observation balloons based at Ross Field, now Arcadia County Park. The gray airships were called "elephants" because of the oxygen-filled "ears" which stabilized them.

The U.S. Army Balloon School was created on the site of Lucky Baldwin's race track, which had closed in 1909. Baldwin's daughter Anita conveyed 185 acres to the U.S. War Department for a balloon training center. Stables were converted to barracks and storerooms. The Army added officers' quarters, machine shops, and a hospital, while a city reservoir became the camp swimming pool.

By 1918 there were 8 of the hydrogen-filled airships and 3,500 men assigned to the school. These soldiers were known as "the eyes of the Army" in World War I. Their job was to search for enemy gun emplacements and relay the information to artillery posts below.

Strange to say, these balloons did not float free. They were tethered to heavy military vehicles and controlled by a ground crew. Two-man teams of observers (a sighter and a radio man) were suspended in 4' by 4' wicker baskets. The balloons could rise to 3,500 feet above ground and stay up as long as four hours.

It took a team of 60 men to raise and lower a balloon, including hoisters, the gas experts (in charge of buoyancy), electricians (for radio telephones to the ground), rippers (to repair the balloons), and "bombers" who set off smoke bombs around the San Gabriel Valley to simulate enemy gunfire. Mirror flashes from the ground also imitated gunfire.

And the scene below? Years later the soldiers recalled orange groves in neat squares, like a polka-dotted patchwork. Roads threaded off into the distance like ribbons, and the little towns of Sierra Madre and Monrovia were tucked into the foothills.

One winter half the balloons were blown away by a fierce storm, one falling in the San Gabriel River wash, another out of the state. In 1918, some of the camp's soldiers died in a flu epidemic, while others convalesced at the old Maryland Hotel in Pasadena.

The first of the balloon companies went to France in December 1917. 30 companies eventually went, and more were ready when armistice was declared in November of 1918.

The old Ross Field was an eyesore by 1935, when an act of Congress allowed the War Department to sell the land to Los Angeles County (at about $300 per acre). The County was required by law to use the land forever only for recreational purposes.

President Franklin D. Roosevelt's Works Progress Administration (WPA) built a baseball diamond with stone bleachers, tennis courts, an 18-hole golf course, swimming pool and picnic grounds in the new County park, where the "elephants" had once soared.

How to get there: The Park is along Huntington Drive at Santa Anita Ave. From the 210 Freeway, exit at Santa Anita Ave. and drive south. Call the Arcadia Historical Society at (626) 446-8512.

Durrell House

⬧ *Azusa* ⬧

AZUSA HAS ONE of the most intriguing names in our region. Could it mean, according to an old joke, "everything from A to Z in the USA"? No, the place owes its name to its early inhabitants.

The Native Americans called Gabrielinos had a settlement known as Asuksa-gna, near the point where the San Gabriel River rushes out of the mountains. Until well into the twentieth century, the river flowed free, sometimes resembling surf when it reached flood stage.

Historian Hugo Reid, in his 1852 article on Southern California Indians, identified the location of Asuksa-gna with present-day Azusa. Over the years many stone implements were found in the region, indicating long habitation.

The first non-natives in the area reported that Asuksa meant "skunk." The ending "-gna" meant place or location (you see it also in Topanga, Cucamonga, Tujunga). The "skunk" label is no insult,

just a recognition of the nocturnal browser still common in gardens along the foothills.

The first definite record of the place was in 1841, when Don Luis Arenas petitioned the town council of Los Angeles for a league of land to the west of the "El Susa" or "the Azusa." Later the Rancho Azusa belonged to Henry Dalton, whose name remains in Big Dalton Canyon above Glendora.

Ranching days changed forever with the advent of the Santa Fe Railroad in 1886 and incorporation of the town in 1889. Nineteenth-century buildings, including a proud Azusa Hotel, came and went—the pace of change seemed to roll on unhindered like the mountain river just to the west of town. Many of the early landmarks were lost.

But the city's historical fortunes have taken a turn for the better, thanks to the Durrell House and the Azusa Historical Society. Moses T. Durrell (rhymes with squirrel) came to the area in the early 1920s and built a substantial house for his wife and five daughters. He did well with his orange groves and served as mayor of the city. After his last daughter lived into old age in the family home, the proposed widening of Foothill Boulevard seemed to spell its doom.

Then land developers gave the house to the city for a historical museum. Moved and resettled behind the City Hall, the five-bedroom, two-story house at that point needed every kind of repair.

Today the Durrell House is well painted and restored, its ample cupboards and closets gathering items from Azusa's past. You will see a photograph of the river at full surge, maps and portraits, natural artifacts from the San Gabriel Canyon, and many items vital in every home before World War II. "We need a barn now!," say the Azusa Historical Society volunteers, echoing the wish of history-savers everywhere.

How to get there: The Durrell House is just north of Azusa City Hall at 213 E. Foothill Blvd. From the 210 Freeway, drive north on Azusa Ave. (Highway 39) to Foothill, and right to City Hall. Turn left on Alameda Ave. to reach the house. For information, call (626) 812-5200.

Puente Largo Railroad Bridge
✧ *Duarte* ✧

THE SAN GABRIEL is the Old Man River of our valley. Its powerful surge underlies this region's history like a living force. It has sustained Indian villages, watered pioneer citrus groves, and flooded the first San Gabriel Mission site, forcing the padres to retreat to higher ground in 1775—to the present Mission in San Gabriel.

The river changed its course at will in the old days, raging in winter storms, meandering in summer over its gravelly bed brought down from the high canyons. Geologists call both the San Gabriel and Los Angeles Rivers "antecedent streams," meaning they existed before the local mountains were uplifted.

Across this contentious and beautiful river, Henry Huntington looked in 1905, wanting to extend his Pacific Electric Line to Azusa and Glendora. A bridge was needed—to carry freight and passenger trains between Los Angeles and the east coast, and also to provide inter-urban service for Southland towns.

By 1907 the Puente Largo Bridge was complete, one of the first steel reinforced concrete arch railroad bridges in the U.S. Its 1,026-foot length was strong enough to carry the heaviest trains and high enough to clear the deepest floods. Its Spanish name means "Long Bridge," but locally it was called the Great Bridge.

The earliest railroad bridges in the U.S. were built with masonry arches, using techniques from 2,000-year old Roman spans. Concrete construction reinforced with steel was a breakthrough developed in the late nineteenth century.

The Puente Largo has 18 reinforced concrete arches, made of 15,000 tons of concrete and 250 tons of steel. The roadbed is 24.5 feet wide, to accommodate two tracks. Vertical slots in the piers held power poles for the electric railway.

The bridge has survived earthquakes and floods, although three piers at the west end washed out in the monster storm of March 1938 and four spans collapsed into the river. Steel girders and wooden beams replaced the missing sections.

The Puente Largo carried the Red Cars between 1907 and 1951. For years, it inspired Duarte High School physics students in traditional bridge building contests. It was known as the finest bridge in the Pacific Electric system.

But the graceful structure which had outlasted storms and quakes finally faced the abandonment of the rail lines, then neglect and vandalism. Barricades and no-trespassing signs offered meager protection.

In 1989 the bridge was renovated by Los Angeles County and the City of Duarte as part of the system of bicycle trails along the San Gabriel River. Today you can walk or bike across the famed span, to experience the ancient river below. No concrete channel here. Take your time, and you may see herons in the lush growth along gravelly sandbars, especially in the early morning or evening.

How to get there: For information, call or visit the Duarte Historical Museum, across the street from the bridge at 777 Encanto Parkway (626) 357-9419. From the 605 Freeway, exit on Huntington Drive, travel east to Encanto, then north to the museum and bridge.

Centennial Heritage Park

◇ *Glendora* ◇

WHAT CAN YOU do with several hundred sooty smudge pots, relics of Southern California's historic citrus years? With imagination, humor and a vision, a Glendora citizens group used the pots to save some of their own history.

"Everyone seemed to want one," recalls Jane Negley, founder of the Glendora Presevation Foundation (GPF). Use of the smoky pots has long been prohibited for heating fruit trees when frost threatens. But hoping to save a historic house and recreate a citrus grove for today's children, GPF raised $12,000 from selling the pots at $15 and $25 each, beginning in 1986. By 1988, they were ready to relocate the Fenton/Sellers/Hamilton House, a Queen Anne style Victorian farmhouse from Glendora's pioneer days. It was facing the bulldozer at approximately 100 years old.

GPF obtained from the City a plot of land along Big Dalton Wash, at the north edge of the 191-acre South Hills Park, a woodsy natural

preserve. Their 7-acre plot had been a dump and was deep in miscellaneous debris, with precious little soil for the proposed new orchard.

House-movings can be dramatic and fun. In March of 1988, the Hamilton House, with its five rooms and two porches, rolled across the flood control channel to the park on a "bridge" made of steel I-beams. Volunteers cleared the dump, adding fresh soil and planting 60 small citrus trees donated by Monrovia Nurseries.

The little farmhouse was built by Glendora founder George Whitcomb and the townspeople for the widow Fenton and her children, whose house had been destroyed by fire. The house contains living room, parlor, and bedroom, with bathroom and porch enclosure added in 1915. Its contents are authentic and touchingly simple, like a tiny high-button shoe found in the walls during restoration. Volunteers stripped 9-12 layers of wallpaper and removed the ancient horsehair-type plaster, once used to prevent cracking.

The park holds another historic building too: the Englehart Workshop, built before the turn of the century, where Orton Englehart invented the famed Rainbird Sprinkler. Brought to the park in pieces, the workshop now displays a variety of early mechanical stuff. The tools were once taken on tour by the American Society of Agricultural Engineering.

On the three undeveloped acres, GPF hopes to add a barn, an early photo studio, a print shop for their 1890s press, domestic gardens—and perhaps more houses to save.

The park presents a Pumpkin Festival each October, and invites school groups and the public to reserve its picnic tables under sheltering oaks.

How to get there: Centennial Heritage Park is at the east end of Mauna Loa Ave. From the 210 Freeway, turn north on Grand Ave., then east on Mauna Loa to the Park. Contact the Glendora Preservation Foundation at (626) 335-2078.

Pioneer Bougainvilleas
⬧ *Glendora* ⬧

IT ALL BEGAN with the French navigator Louis Antoine de Bougainville, who lived from 1729 to 1811. After traveling to Canada and the Falkland Islands, he made a trip around the world (1767-69) accompanied by astronomers and naturalists. His name was given to Bougainville, a large volcanic island in the southwest Pacific, now part of Papua New Guinea. And his name was given to the bougain- villea vine.

This tropical woody vine is a common sight in the Southland. Its petal-like bracts show vibrant colors ranging from purple and red to magenta, orange, pink, or white. The *Sunset Garden Book* lists 34 varieties common in Southern California. These plants love heat, and they take off with thorny exuberance. But you have not seen bougainvilleas until you have seen the bougainvilleas of Glendora.

This special planting has been declared a California Registered His- torical Landmark. 24 individual plants grow along two sides of a city

block, once the property of R. W. Hamlin and occupied by his orange groves. Together, this is the largest growth of bougainvillea in the United States. Interspersed with tall palms, the vines toss bright magenta bracts to a height of 70 feet (tamed by occasional trimming).

Within each plant is a giant "trellis" of metal poles and rings, to keep the vines from overpowering the sidewalk. Left unchecked, they would drape into the street as well.

The origin of these beauties presents some historical controversy. The Landmark plaque, placed by the State in 1978, declares they were planted in 1901 by Hamlin, from parent stock brought to California on a whaling ship about 1870. But some Glendora citizens clearly remember the planting of the vines in the 1930's.

Long-time residents report different memories. Some recall walking by them on the way to school in the '20s, or pulling a baseball out of their thorny clutches during a childhood street game. Others are sure the vines were not there until the '30s.

One fact on the marker is beyond question: the vines are one of the best remaining examples of the early twentieth century image of California as a paradise. Southern California, where everything seemed to grow and climbing roses covered entire cottages, was especially known as a new Eden.

The best way to see the bougainvilleas is on foot, walking around the block bounded by Bennett, Cullen, Whitcomb, and Minnesota. The vines are along Minnesota and Bennett. Within the walls, on the old citrus property, there are now attractive condominiums known as Rancho del Bougainvillea.

Surprising but true, even in early winter these monumental plants may have lots of color, although the warm seasons are most promising for bloom. It's worth a detour to see these botanical landmarks.

How to get there: From the 210 Freeway, exit at Grand Ave. and drive north to Bennett Ave., then right to Minnesota Ave. Contact the Glendora Historical Museum at (626) 963-0419 for further information.

Hamlin House
DAR Headquarters
✧ *Glendora* ✧

RUBEN AND HELEN Hamlin had no children in their spacious family-sized Glendora house, built in 1909—yet it is now home to about 10,000 daughters. These are members of the California State Society of the Daughters of the American Revolution (the DAR), headquartered today in the Hamlin House.

The national DAR was founded in 1890 in Washington D.C., and the California State Society formed immediately, in 1891. The organization's themes of education, patriotism, and historic preservation fit neatly into the Hamlins' home, well suited to hospitality and research.

The Hamlins created their Southern California home in stages, within the original township of Glendora. Their builder, Charles Mace of Azusa, first constructed a carriage house (1905) which is still at

the back of the property. Here the Hamlins lived while a two story pre-cut house was being assembled for them across Bennett Avenue. Such a house, with numbered pieces, could be ordered from the East at that time and sent to California for about $1,000. (It's still in place too). In that house they lived until the large Craftsman-style dwelling was finally ready for them.

Natural elements are featured in the big house, including rock from the San Gabriel River, hand wrought iron, and abundant wood. The entrance porch is solidly anchored with stonework. Visitors step through a surprisingly wide door which is oak on the outside and pine on the inside. However, the paneling and beams of the house depart from the Craftsman ideal of natural wood; instead they are dark, more to the Victorian taste.

The interior contains many historical references, including carvings of native California wood depicting Father Junipero Serra and a Revolutionary War soldier. The dining room displays commemorative plates with events of the Revolution, and a Lady Liberty quilt, hanging on a wall, carries on the theme.

A working part of the house is the library in a sunny den. It contains books and periodicals used for genealogical research, and more are stored in the large basement. The library is open by arrangement.

After her husband's death in 1939, Mrs. Hamlin lived on in the house until 1961. Following several other owners, the Daughters purchased the property in 1982 to serve as their California Headquarters. The upstairs bedrooms have housed many visiting State Officers, and a comfortable screened sleeping porch is nearby. The closet of the master bedroom hides a "secret room". Like the children who found a fantasy world by stepping through a wardrobe, you emerge into a snug dormer room just under the roof. No one would know it was there.

Framed by palms and California live oaks, this house has become a headquarters, but it remains a home.

How to get there: The Hamlin House is at 201 West Bennett Ave. From the 210 Freeway, exit at Grand Ave. and drive north; turn right on Bennett. For information and tours, call (626) 963-1776.

Russian Orthodox Church
✧ *Glendora* ✧

QUIET SEEMS TO linger around St. Andrews Orthodox Church, a tiny white stucco sanctuary next to the South Hills. Few are aware of its origins and history, but it was once at the heart of Glendora's Russian Community.

In 1952, the American Friends Service Committee (a Quaker organization) sponsored the settlement of refugees in California, under the Displaced Persons Act of 1948. A colony of Russians called "Our Home" was established in Glendora, originally 48 people who built their houses on 17 acres of the old Blackwood Ranch.

Bobbie Battler, Glendora historian, recalls that group members lived in a local farm house as they arrived until their homes were ready. Structures from a Japanese Relocation Center in Arizona were dismantled when their occupants returned home, and the lumber was bought for the Russian settlement.

The men arrived first at the Glendora colony and sent for their families later. They came on sponsorships for citrus picking and joined that thriving industry. Climbing a 14-foot ladder with a 50-pound bag of fruit was an essential requirement for the work.

Life was good for the newcomers. A special U.S. Census showed Glendora's population as under 6,000 that first year. The setting was rural, and low hills gathered closely around the Russian families and their groves.

Orthodox religious services were held in a community building, and the present church was completed in 1958. The community followed the orthodox principle of "using things of the world in worship"—lamps, candles and icons enriched the little sanctuary, within its simple exterior. A school of the Russian language was conducted there for a while. Extending their hospitality, one family had as many as 39 foreign students from 19 different countries living in its home over the years.

But eventually the community dispersed, and few descendents of the Russian Colony live near the church now. The church building is no longer used and it remains locked. Reminders of the area's past survive in the street names: Cossacks Place, Saint Vladimir, Zara, and Steffen Streets.

Stopping on Cossacks Place today, you'll find the whitewashed church amidst small trees. An image of St. Andrew, holding his X-shaped cross, hangs in the arched doorway. The building doesn't have the traditional dome, but tall windows along the nave are topped with onion-dome-shaped cutouts.

Behind the church, a monument supports the orthodox cross with its three bars. In Russian and English, the inscription reads: "In memory of victims of forced repatriation, 1945." The future of the little building is uncertain.

"Our Home" once provided a safe haven from the turmoil of World War II aftermath. Although the colonists are gone now and so is the citrus culture that supported them, you'll sense a little flame of memory at Glendora's Russian Orthodox Church.

How to get there: The church is at 1431 Cossacks Place. From the 210 Freeway, exit at Grand Ave. and drive north; turn right on Alosta Ave., left on Compromise Line Road which becomes Saint Vladimir St., and right on Cossacks Place.

La Fetra Center

✧ *Glendora* ✧

"BOULDER GRANGE"—it sounds like a name out of an English novel, but you'll see it suits this rambling mansion of Glendora, with the river rock foundation and fireplaces. Now it is called the La Fetra Center for Seniors.

The house was built about 1904 for the Brandholdt family. It's in solid Craftsman style, with varied windows, a gable over the doorway, a sheltered porch and stone piers. Glendora was new then, born of the real estate boom in the 1880's. The town was surrounded by orange and lemon groves.

Right around 1904, several events affected life at Boulder Grange. Telephone service was new in 1902. The Pacific Electric Railway extended its line to Glendora in 1907, to much celebration. There the Red Cars had their turn-around, heading back to Los Angeles. Electric power came to Glendora homes in 1908 and gas lines in 1909. This must have been one of the most substantial houses when the city was incorporated in 1911.

As the city grew and the groves disappeared, the mansion was sold in 1940 for apartments and later a bed and breakfast inn. The Pacific Electric ended its Glendora run in 1951, and the citrus industry was gone by 1956. Finally in 1989, divided into eight apartments, the mansion had outlived its early years. It seemed too large, too old to carry on much longer.

But hope was in sight. The Ludwick and La Fetra families of Glendora bought and donated the property to the City of Glendora, to be the La Fetra Center for Seniors. Although the La Fetras had never lived here, the mansion was given this name to commemorate a pioneer family of the town.

The brothers Lawson and Milton La Fetra had come to Glendora in 1885 and built a Victorian mansion now gone. Later four more La Fetra brothers and a sister arrived, and they assisted founder George D. Whitcomb in establishing the new town and its water supply.

Clement and Mary La Fetra took their own place in Glendora history when they began manufacturing in 1935 the famed sprinkler known as Rainbird, invented by Clement's cousin Orton Englehart. Clement lived to 1963, and Mary carried on as president of Rainbird until 1977. In 1982 she inspired senior citizens in Glendora and anywhere else by completing her B.A. degree in History at Pomona College.

The house that now honors Clement and Mary still has its stone fireplaces, pocket doors, and mellow woodwork. A 10,000 square foot new wing, harmonious in design, was opened in December 1997. This is not a residence, but a gathering place for daily use.

The La Fetra Center holds many classes, activities, and clubs. The old "grange" is busier than it ever was, a building with its roots down into Glendora history.

How to get there: The Center is at 333 E. Foothill Blvd. From the 210 Freeway, exit at Grand Ave. and drive north; turn right on Foothill. Call (626) 914-0560.

Monrovia Municipal Plunge
Monrovia Historical Museum
✧ *Monrovia* ✧

SOUTHERN CALIFORNIA IS dotted with buildings that began with one use, then changed to another. This metamorphosis is sometimes as strange as caterpillar to butterfly. Other times a new use just updates the old.

The Monrovia Municipal Plunge, created 75 years ago, is no more. But its building and site still form a recreation center, holding community events where youngsters once met for watery hijinks.

At the end of 1885, William Monroe (originally of Soap Creek, Iowa) and four other men owned land purchased from Lucky Baldwin's Rancho Santa Anita. Monroe had come west to help Charles Crocker build railroads, work which eventually took him to Chile, Alaska, and throughout California.

The five friends pooled their 489 acres and launched a new town in 1886. It was named for founder William Monroe and its Myrtle Street was named for his eldest daughter.

The community was focused along the Santa Fe Railroad and later Route 66, "America's Main Street", which runs through the city. In the prosperous 1920s Monrovia purchased 22 acres for a park. Someone remembered the old reservoirs among foothill orange groves which used to be the town's swimming holes. A municipal plunge seemed just the thing for the times.

In 1925 the spacious new building was complete, a two-story central portion with single-story wings at each side, in the popular Spanish Colonial Revival style. Boys' dressing rooms occupied one wing, girls' the other. Beyond the arched lobby was an Olympic size sparkling pool.

Monrovians enjoyed the plunge for over fifty years, but finally both building and pool needed major structural repairs. What to do with this summertime Mecca, so woven into community memories? At last the pool was abandoned, and a new one built at Monrovia High School.

But the town's Centennial in 1986 was just the chance for reviving the site. The Monrovia Historical Museum now occupies the old building. You'll see photographs of how the aging walls were rebuilt. After all was shored up, the original Spanish tiles were installed as a new roof.

Today the museum serves as the community's "attic", although far better organized than childhood attics you may remember. The fun of such a place is in its details. You'll see a telephone switchboard from the solar water heater company of 1909 (ahead of its time) which became the Day and Night Company.

Another display shows the Pottenger Sanatorium, founded 1903, when Monrovia was a health center famous for its climate. Note the model of the building, now gone, and such remedies as mustard plasters. And you can leaf through Pacific Electric Magazine copies from the 20s, 30s, and 40s.

The former pool is now a large courtyard and garden, used for meetings and festivities, drawing people together as in the old days.

How to get there: The museum is at 742 East Lemon Ave. From the 210 Freeway, exit at Mountain Ave., drive north, and turn left at Lemon. Call (626) 357-9537.

Anderson House

✧ *Monrovia* ✧

"IT KEEPS COMING back like a song…" Several communities in Southern California have a special house from the 1880s, restored and ready to visit. They seem almost like sister houses, full of similarities, yet each distinctly itself.

The George H. Anderson House in Monrovia is one of these. Probably built in 1886, it matches almost to the year the Bailey House in Whittier, the Doctors' House in Glendale, and several houses at Heritage Square along the Pasadena Freeway.

John and Lizzie Anderson came West from Ohio just as W. N. Monroe and his associates were founding Monrovia in 1886. Mrs. Anderson returned briefly to Ohio for the birth of her son George, coming back when he was four months old. From that return until his death in 1974 at age 88, George Anderson lived in the family home on East Lime Avenue.

His life's work was as a banker in Monrovia. An avid outdoorsman, "he knew the local mountain country like the back of his hand," recalled Monrovia historian T. M. Hotchkiss. His brother Louis was adventurous too, and later became forest supervisor of the Cleveland National Forest near San Diego.

After the death of George, who never married, the house was acquired by the Monrovia Historical Society which was formed to receive it.

The house contains many community keepsakes, given by families in town. There is no museum feeling here—just a household which naturally contains things like kidskin hair curlers, a combination gas and electric light fixture, and a pump organ. You're a guest, so you're welcome to sit down and play it.

The house has twelve foot ceilings, a broad central hall, parlor and dining room separated by pocket doors, three bedrooms with an amiable clutter, and a kitchen with a wood-burning range. Externally, its style is Queen Anne, with an asymmetrical plan and decorative woodwork. A part of the original barn remains, as well as two oak trees in the back, planted by John Anderson just a hammock's-distance apart.

"The more you look, the more you see." Going from room to room, you'll see little collections that invite comparisons as you go along. Quilts, for one thing; also clocks. The local Mormons painted and embroidered a modern quilt with iris, Monrovia's city flower. Another quilt is stitched to show 16 historic buildings from Monrovia's centennial in 1986, while a nineteenth-century quilt is bright as a peacock, made from silk party dresses.

And the clocks—this is often a beloved family object handed down. You'll find half a dozen intriguing ones at the Anderson House. The kitchen is full of "what is that??" items, once necessities at the heart of the household.

How to get there: The Anderson House is at 215 East Lime Ave. From the 210 Freeway, exit at Myrtle Ave., drive north, then right on Lime Ave. Call the Monrovia Historical Society at (626) 358-0803.

Aztec Hotel

✧ *Monrovia* ✧

IT WAS ONE-OF-A-KIND when it was built in 1925. The Aztec Hotel in Monrovia was opened with much pride, then led a precarious life but still survives today.

The 1920s were a time of optimism and high spirits. This shows in architecture all over the Southland. In Monrovia, tourist travel was lively along Route 66 (Foothill Boulevard). But in those boom times the city suffered from having no large tourist hotel.

Local businessmen had tried to finance a hotel resembling cliff dwellings, with hogans for guest houses, but this plan fell through. Then in 1923, Monrovia citizens approached the Hockenberry System, a hotel financing organization of the East. That company launched a fund-raising campaign in town with a community banquet in the social parlors of the Methodist Church.

120 civic leaders set out to sell stock in the venture, with daily free lunches for the rival teams. In just three months, the campaign closed with pledges totalling $138,900.

Robert Stacy-Judd of Hollywood was chosen as architect. The hotel's design, he stated, was not really Aztec but Mayan. The name "Aztec" would be used because the public was more familiar with that term. Stacy-Judd believed that pre-Columbian Revival architecture, since it was "native American," should become the true American style in the future.

He wrote a detailed description of the hotel's interior, where he improvised freely on Mayan themes. The entry vestibule had mural paintings with symbols of Mayan culture and warfare. Carved stone effects bordered the walls and ceilings. The arch from vestibule to lobby was like carved Chinese arches, a universal style (he believed) from Asia to Central America. In the lobby paintings, the sun god and the god of lust added an exotic presence.

The Aztec had a brief heyday. Its grand opening was well covered by the press. The ornate facade attracted attention from Route 66 travelers. Sunday dinner for $1.25 at the Aztec was a highlight in the 1920s.

But by 1938 the hotel was not making money. One historian asked, was it too fantastic in appearance for success? The hotel closed, then re-opened in the 1940s. Checkered fortunes continued, and in 1983 the Aztec was for sale again.

Each time the building survived, but gradually its original wild spirit was trimmed back. The interior murals all but disappeared. The west end of the lobby was pre-empted for a restaurant-bar. Small shops came and went within the frontage of the hotel. Incongruous signs wrecked the Mayan unity of the design. Today the building contains weekly rental housing.

But at least, it's still there. We have not lost the Aztec Hotel. And despite its altered state, the Aztec still conveys that dash of the bizarre from the spirited 1920s.

How to get there: The Aztec is at 311 W. Foothill Blvd. From the 210 Freesay, exit at Myrtle Ave. and drive north; turn left on Foothill. For further information, consult the Monrovia Public Library: (626) 358-0174.

Chinese Courtyard Garden
Pacific Asia Museum
◇ *Pasadena* ◇

A CHINESE COURTYARD garden is like a Chinese landscape painting come alive, but this time in three dimensions. Stone, water and plants make a new composition from every angle.

The courtyard garden of Pasadena's Pacific Asia Museum is hidden away in a Chinese palace-style building, its architecture dating from the Han dynasty (206 B.C. to 220 A.D.) The serene garden is just steps away from hurrying traffic on Los Robles Avenue. It resembles the Ming garden in New York's Metropolitan Museum of Art, but that one is entirely indoors.

The palace is the former home of Grace Nicholson, who came to California from Philadelphia in 1901. First a collector of American Indian artifacts, she later devoted herself to Oriental art. In 1929 her

Chinese treasure house, designed by the firm of Marston, Van Pelt and Maybury, was complete, and she lived there until her death in 1948. Later the building was home to the Pasadena Art Museum; then in 1971 it became the Pacific Asia Museum, devoted to the arts of Asia and the Pacific.

The present courtyard garden was created in 1979, though its tallest trees date from Grace Nicholson's day. Plant life there mixes the familiar with the rare. The ginkgo tree shows bright yellow leaves in autumn, and the goldenrain tree (commonly grown near temples in China) has showy buff-colored pods in the winter.

Large porous limestone rocks in the courtyard symbolize mountains. Although similar to traditional ones from China's Lake Tai, these came from a fossilized lake bed in Kansas. The two largest are named Flying Horse and Yin/Yang.

Water is vital in Chinese gardens; it moves and it reflects the sky. Here the visitor sits by a small pool where bright colored koi stir lazily. Flowers are not of major importance, but there is a big shrub rose, azaleas (called little cuckoo flower by the Chinese), camellias (native to China), and wisteria. Chrysanthemums and cymbidiums are brought into the courtyard as the seasons allow.

Two handsome marble lion-dogs, male and female, guard the central outdoor staircase. Other mythical beasts are the little deer with fish scales, colorful ceramic dogs at the roofline, and dragons carved around the many doors and windows. On a stone bench sits the Young Prince, a child-sized bronze figure, in the Confucian garb of a scholar official. He often holds a fresh flower in his folded hands.

Nearby is an elegant tray landscape, an arrangement of slate imitating mountains, set in a marble tray to contain water. The piece is named Yi Kong Shi Bi—Rocks Leaning Against the Sky.

All around the courtyard are decorative motifs from the plant kingdom: lotus, peony, and the cloud-shaped fungus called the plant of immortality. The Chinese courtyard garden, shady in summer and open to the sky in winter, invites your visit in any season.

How to get there: The Pacific Asia Museum is at 46 N. Los Robles Avenue. From the 210 Freeway, exit at Los Robles and drive south. Call (626) 449-2742.

La Casita del Arroyo
✧ *Pasadena* ✧

FROM THE SAN GABRIEL MOUNTAINS, through Pasadena and South Pasadena, then west beside Highland Park until it meets the Los Angeles River, runs the Arroyo Seco. This picturesque natural area was once the center of the Craftsman movement in the West. Today the spirit of that time can be felt in Pasadena's La Casita del Arroyo (the Little House of the Arroyo).

This little club house was dedicated in 1933, after just four months of construction. It was built to relieve unemployment during the Depression and to provide a community meeting place on the brink of the Arroyo.

The noted architect Myron Hunt contributed his design and supervised the work without charge. His other Southern California buildings include the Pasadena Public Library, the Huntington Art Gallery and Library, parts of Occidental College and the Bridges Hall of Music ("Little Bridges") at Pomona College. La Casita was a present to the region where his architecture had flourished.

The house ingeniously used salvaged materials. The walls were of boulders carried up from the streambed below. Roof shakes were cut from fallen trees in the upper canyon. Almost all the lumber came from the old bicycle track built at the Rose Bowl for the 1932 Olympic Games of Los Angeles.

Andirons for the fireplace were forged from discarded street car rails. The project, a classic example of "found materials," was a joint effort of the City of Pasadena and the Pasadena Garden Club (founded 1916).

But an arson fire in 1985 gutted the little house. The City restored it to the original design, and the Pasadena Garden Club rallied to the cause with a new landscape design by Isabelle Greene and Yosh Befu. The Club now faithfully maintains the garden.

Today La Casita is used almost daily for meetings, receptions, and City functions. It contains a main assembly room, with windows overlooking the Arroyo, a small kitchen, and storage areas. Outside terraces give a vista north to the graceful Colorado Street Bridge, built in 1913.

Groups and individuals may reserve the building, with priority given to Pasadena-based community service and non-profit organizations, and to City-sponsored events.

Open to all who stroll by, is the new Water Conservation Garden. Plants with very different water requirements grow in three sections: "water consuming," "water conserving," and "super water saving." Each has a different meter to record water use.

Notice the permeable paving that replaces conventional parking—it's irregular sidewalk fragments with green herbs filling in. Nearby an old oak has young saplings grafted in around its base, to regenerate the tree and defeat oak root fungus. This is "in-arch grafting," and it gives the weakened tree a second chance. It's just another way of joining new life to old traditions at La Casita del Arroyo.

How to get there: La Casita del Arroyo is at 177 So. Arroyo Blvd. From the 210 Freeway, drive south on Fair Oaks Ave., right on California Blvd., and right on Arroyo Blvd. Call (626) 744-7275 to inquire about reservations.

Vista del Arroyo Hotel

◇ *Pasadena* ◇

THE MORNING ROOM and the Sunset Room catch the first and last sunlight of the day, stirring up memories in Pasadena's Vista del Arroyo Hotel. Although the historic building now holds the Ninth Circuit Federal Court of Appeals, its uses have ranged from winter resort to wartime healthcare.

It was the California sunshine that brought people to the site in the first place. In 1882 Mrs. Emma Bangs built the Arroyo Vista Guest House there, for Eastern and Midwestern visitors on winter retreats. Her wide porches overlooked the stream bed far below and the San Rafael Hills to the west.

Arrival of the Santa Fe railroad in 1886 spurred Pasadena's great resort era, with expanding hotels and eminent guests. After Mrs. Bangs' death in 1903, the Vista had several owners including Daniel Linnard, the proprietor of San Francisco's Fairmont and San Diego's Hotel Del Coronado. In 1913 the curving Colorado Street Bridge was finished, crossing the Arroyo just to the north.

By 1920 the early wood-frame guest houses were gone. A Mediterranean style main building replaced them, designed by architects Marston and Van Pelt. A decade later George Wiemeyer created a six-story addition, with its landmark tower, loggia and ballroom. The Vista del Arroyo was complete with 400 guest rooms on twelve acres of land.

During the Depression, the Vista kept up a brave style with summer suppers on the lawn and the "talkies" shown in the banquet hall. The Army took over the entire property in 1943 under the War Powers Act and converted the hotel to the McCornack Army Hospital. After 1949, the once proud Vista was "surplus property," used only occasionally by the government for the next thirty years.

But a better fate was at hand. Chief Judge Richard Chambers arranged for the Ninth Circuit Court of Appeals to occupy the Vista. After a $10.8 million renovation, the building was re-dedicated in 1986. A Presidential Design Award from the National Endowment for the Arts followed.

There are three courtrooms on the main floor: small, medium, and large. Each has decorative tile, window detail, or grillwork (some is fiberglass replacement, provided by Hollywood set designers during the restoration). The hotel's main dining room is now the Law Library. Off the main lobby, the Court Clerk's Office occupies the former sun lounge.

In the east-facing Morning Room are witty landscape murals by Terry Schoonhoven, who also painted skies in the Plaza Pasadena shopping mall. Tall cactus plants stand like a cast of characters for the murals.

To the west, the Sunset Room catches a few rays, opening onto the veranda with its dazzling view. Neatly enough, the 134 Freeway bridge is hidden behind the nearer Colorado Street Bridge, leaving undisturbed a classic Pasadena vista.

How to get there: The Courthouse is at 125 S. Grand Ave. From the 134 Freeway exit on Orange Grove and drive south, turn right on Maylin St., then right on Grand. Call (626) 583-7019 for information and the possibility of docent tours.

Pasadena Playhouse
✧ *Pasadena* ✧

THE FIRST LANDMARK to be declared by Pasadena's Cultural Heritage Committee, the Pasadena Playhouse is worthy of an afternoon pilgrimage—to pick up some tickets and sit a while in one of the city's prettiest courtyards.

The building was created by architect Elmer Grey in the Spanish Revival style, for a May opening night in 1925. Red tile roof, creamy stucco and cloistered arcades speak of early California Mission days. The well-proportioned building has wings for a little shop and a restaurant, and the flagstone courtyard is fringed with olive and palm trees. A fancy tiled fountain and historic markers also attract our attention.

The founding spirit of the place was Gilmor Brown, raised on a North Dakota farm, who came to Pasadena in 1917 at age 30. Actor and producer, he established the Community Players and soon was

staging as many as two shows a month. On a surge of popularity, the new playhouse was budgeted at $300,000 and constructed by the same company which had built Grauman's Egyptian Theatre. Stylish first-nighters attended for $5 per ticket.

In 1936 the six-floor tower building was added, with an outdoor basketball court on the roof. With this rehearsal and costume space, offices, and the emerging drama school, the Pasadena Playhouse became one of the largest theater complexes in the world.

In its first 25 years, the Playhouse produced 1,348 plays, including all 37 Shakespeare plays. 500 productions were American or World premieres. In 1937, the State Legislature named the Playhouse the State Theatre of California, for having brought "national and international renown to our state."

The School of Theatre Arts opened there in 1928 and was an illustrious spot for several decades. Among its alumni were Dustin Hoffman and Gene Hackman, while the mainstage productions featured William Holden, Tyrone Power, Martha Graham, Eve Arden, and hundreds more. Those were glory days.

Gilmor Brown died in 1960, and already changing times were swirling around his enterprise. The advent of television, the new Los Angeles Music Center, changes in Pasadena all threatened the future of the Playhouse. The mainstage went dark. Costumes for king, queen, bride, and pirate were sold at auction.

But the melodrama turned for the better with financing and restoration which eventually led to the Playhouse of today. Once again audiences enjoy intermission coffee under the stars in the courtyard which has seen so many stylish crowds.

True to form, the Playhouse is still planning firsts, as regional theaters are often the sources of new work and adventurous programming. If you want to be in the action yourself, the Friends of the Playhouse welcome volunteers for ushering, cooking for the actors, or other projects.

How to get there: The Playhouse is at 37 So. El Molino Ave. From the 210 Freeway, exit at Lake Ave., drive south to Colorado Blvd., right on Colorado and left on El Molino. For tickets or to inquire about the Friends, call (626) 356-7529

Friendship Baptist Church
✧ *Pasadena* ✧

"ON THE NATIONAL REGISTER of Historic Places": this does not mean just a pretty face. To receive this recognition, a building or place must have major significance in the life and fabric of a community. Such a landmark is the Friendship Baptist Church of Pasadena.

Dr. Hiram Reid, in his 1895 *History of Pasadena*, reports little churches and religious societies springing up like seedlings in the new town. Most of these are gone now. But there in his pages is the Friendship Baptist Church, a Black congregation, organized in 1893. The sixteen members first met in a hall, then held services in a tent as their numbers grew. It was the same year that Colorado Blvd. was first paved and a large bird's-eye view of Pasadena was printed, on view today in the Pasadena Public Library.

In 1923 the church purchased its current site at Dayton and DeLacey Streets. The surrounding neighborhood of bungalows

housed a thriving community of Asian, Black, and Mexican-American families.

Norman Foote Marsh was the architect of the present church building, completed in 1925 at a cost of $100,000. He also designed the canal city of Venice, California, the University of Redlands, Hollywood High School, and other public buildings of the Southland. The first sermon in the new building was preached by the Rev. W. D. Carter, thirteenth pastor of the church who served for 30 years until his retirement at age 90.

Marsh has blended two styles popular in the 1920s, Spanish Colonial Revival and Mission. The stucco facade is edged by a curving gable and features a quatrefoil stained glass window. The square bell tower, with its arched openings, adds a feeling of strength. Along the east wall are three tall stained glass windows, beautiful from the inside with colorings of opal and amethyst.

Decorative details include Spanish baroque doorways and wrought iron lanterns. Marsh had specified: "the materials are to be the best of their several kinds."

Inside is a broad sanctuary seating 600 people, with the Carter chapel holding a further 150. Dr. Martin Luther King, Jr. spoke at the church on four occasions, and his wife Coretta Scott King sang there in 1966.

Over the years the church has maintained active programs, including food distribution, scholarships, and child care. The gospel choir of Friendship Baptist Church radiates joy and a vigor more powerful than solar energy. They take this music far and wide in the community.

Norman Marsh's building, placed on the National Register in 1978, is in a different setting now. The residential surroundings are mostly gone. Just to the north is the newly revived Old Pasadena district. Under guidance of a restoration architect, the building has recently been completely repaired from past earthquake damage. Dr. Reid would be pleased about this enduring church in the life of Pasadena.

How to get there: The church is at 80 W. Dayton St. From the 210 Freeway, exit at Lake Ave., drive south to Del Mar Ave., right to DeLacey Ave., and right to Dayton. Call (626) 793-1062.

Fenyes Mansion
(Pasadena Historical Museum)
✧ *Pasadena* ✧

THERE'S A FAMILY story of four generations in the white Beaux Arts mansion. Today you can visit the house and trace this family, surrounded by their original furniture, paintings and belongings.

The mansion was built in 1905 for Dr. Adalbert Fenyes, a physician of Hungarian descent, and his wife, Eva Scott Fenyes, who was an artist in water colors. Dr. Fenyes was fascinated by entomology and left an important insect collection to the Academy of Sciences in San Francisco.

Architect Robert Farquhar designed the home for this energetic pair. He had studied at the Ecole des Beaux-Arts in Paris, the leading architectural school of that day. In Southern California he also designed the William Andrews Clark Library and the Beverly Hills High School in the 1920s.

For Dr. and Mrs. Fenyes, he created an 18-room neo-classical villa, with arched windows and balustrades. In 1911, an addition was designed by Sylvanus Marston for the north side of the house. This

contained a solarium used as a greenhouse for ferns and orchids, (complete with water trenches and steam heat) and a two-story studio for arts and entertaining—today the most intriguing room in the house.

Musicians, artists, and scientists visited in the early 1900s, and the motion picture industry came to film such stars as Tom Mix and Douglas Fairbanks. The popular "Eleanor and Franklin" was shot on the grounds also.

Mrs. Leonora Curtin, daughter of the Fenyes, lived on in the family home. Her daughter, also named Leonora, married Y.A. Paloheimo of Finland in 1946. When he was appointed Finnish Consul for the Southwest, the white mansion became the Finnish Consulate. The Paloheimos adopted four Finnish war orphans, and thus the fourth generation of the family settled in. Diplomatic and social events at the house had an international flavor for 18 years. Then in 1970, the family donated the mansion and gardens to the Pasadena Historical Society, which maintains them to this day.

Visitors may step into one of the last grand homes remaining on the famous Boulevard. European antique furniture mixes sociably with American paintings and a wealth of clocks. Tiffany lamps glow gently. Lovers of Persian and Turkish carpets will admire examples of Tabriz, Agra, Kerman and other designs.

The studio has a picture gallery, a trapdoor for actors to appear and disappear, and a balcony for musicians. Here Mrs. Fenyes painted and Pasadena's interesting characters mingled over the years.

The mansion has historical displays on the ground floor, showing Pasadena artifacts and photographs (including fine coverage of the Mt. Lowe Railway). A separate building on the grounds, the History Center, holds more exhibits and a library of books, articles and about 700,000 photos and negatives. The mansion also stores over 3,000 pieces of costumes and textiles, a major collection and great fun in special exhibits.

How to get there: The Mansion (Pasadena Historical Museum) is at 470 W. Walnut Street. From the 210 Freeway, exit at Orange Grove Blvd. and drive north. Turn right on Walnut. Call (626) 577-1660.

Landmark Buildings at
Pasadena City College
⬧ *Pasadena* ⬧

AS LANDMARKS OF more than 60 years, three handsome college buildings face a mirror pool and Colorado Boulevard in Pasadena. Few people remember now that they were once named for famous educators: the long central building for Horace Mann, the two side ones for Louis Agassiz to the east and Jane Addams to the west. But these buildings are not what they once were.

Education sprang up on this spot, among neighboring orange groves, in 1912. The architect Norman Marsh designed three rather majestic buildings for the new Pasadena Polytechnic High School, part of the city's public schools. The three-story buildings had fancy cornices, columns, and on the largest, a central tower. A panoramic photo of the original trio hangs in the college president's office.

In 1924 the growing town established Pasadena City Junior College, with 267 students. Then the high school and junior college

shared the Colorado Boulevard campus. But the Long Beach earthquake of 1933 caused such havoc that Mann, Agassiz and Addams all had to be demolished down to their foundations.

More distinguished architects appeared, this time the firm of Bennett, Marston and Maybury. While students attended college in a "city of tents," the firm designed new buildings on the same footprints as the old. They were financed by bond issues and by the Public Works Administration (PWA), one of President Roosevelt's New Deal agencies to provide employment in the Depression.

The new designers created buildings far simpler than the lost ones. Creamy stucco exteriors followed the simple lines of "streamline moderne." Decorative detail was understated: small carvings, or a repeated scallop motif at the rooflines. The three new buildings were complete by 1937. Years later the two mirror pools were added, echoing this stylish simplicity of the 1930s.

That decade was a lively one at the college. The little Astronomy Building was dedicated in 1931 by Albert Einstein. The first airplane built in the public schools, the PCC 1, marked its first flight in 1937.

During World War II many students departed for military enlistments, but a job training program was held at the college for the war effort. In 1947 the school was formally named Pasadena City College. Buildings were steadily added, and in 1955 the college counted 4,000 students and 188 faculty and staff. Today, the student body numbers over 25,000, with about 370 faculty and staff. The campus has expanded to 53 acres with 30 buildings.

The three original buildings (second version) are in their places from 1912, facing the multicultural hum along the boulevard. They are now known more prosaically as C Building (the center), D Building (west) and E Building (east). But the foundations of Mann, Agassiz and Addams are still there, supporting these structures at the heart of PCC.

How to get there: Pasadena City College is at 1570 E. Colorado Blvd. From the 210 Freeway, exit at Hill Ave. (if eastbound) or Allen Ave. (if westbound), and drive south to Colorado. Turn left from Hill or right from Allen. Call (626) 585-7315.

Pasadena Civic Auditorium
✧ *Pasadena* ✧

AN ELEGANT LADY, rather large to be sure, with an Italian accent and memories of Pompeii. How did she get to Pasadena?

It's the Italian accent that might get you, both inside and outside of the Pasadena Civic Auditorium. The building has housed the performing arts for almost seventy years, but it is no doubt a work of art in itself.

The Auditorium is the southernmost building of Pasadena's Civic Center trio, including the City Hall and the Central Library to the north. As early as 1908, leading citizens had called for a city plan. Finally in 1921 George Ellery Hale, director of the Mount Wilson Observatory, gained support for the idea, and the firm of Bennett and Parsons was hired to create a plan.

A juried competition was held for design of the three central buildings, and voters approved a $3.5 million bond issue for the land ac-

quisition and construction. The last of the three structures, the Civic Auditorium, was completed in 1932.

The architects—Bergstrom, Bennett and Haskell—took seriously the planners' recommendation for "architecture of the Renaissance" in the "countries bordering upon the Mediterranean Sea." Their auditorium is on a grand scale, but resembles a simple Italian villa. The first story is rusticated concrete imitating stone, and the second story is colored a light buff. A serene symmetry gives the front a stately air. Blue and gray tiles decorate the window openings, while theatrical masks and crowns to represent the City of Pasadena appear in the arches above.

A marble foyer leads into a scene of Pompeiian exuberance. The auditorium is alive with colors, especially red and supporting shades of buff and terra cotta. Painted decoration covers every surface. A "trompe l'oeil" effect simulates columns and folds on the flat walls. The ceiling is also in Pompeiian style, and the recessed lighting is neatly hidden in the design of garlands. Sitting in the balcony puts this sweep of art right over your head.

All these decorations were designed and painted by John B. Smeraldi, an Italian artist who also did the paintings in the Los Angeles Biltmore Hotel.

In 1979 the Pasadena Civic Center was listed on the National Register of Historic Places. Today there are many occasions to visit the Civic Auditorium, with its seating capacity of 3,059. It is home to the Pasadena Symphony and also hosts other orchestras and dance companies. The Italian crowd of painted figures gives the large space the liveliness of a Roman piazza.

The Gold Room, used for special events and music lectures, and the first floor corridors have coffered ceilings stenciled with Renaissance designs. The Italians knew how to make the most of ceilings. Where else in a room is there such a large unbroken space—a veritable canvas to cover with art?

How to get there: The Civic Auditorium is at 300 E. Green St. From the 210 Freeway, exit at Fair Oaks Ave. and drive south; turn left on Green St. Call (626) 793-2122.

Church of the Angels

◇ *Pasadena* ◇

"SEEKING COMES BEFORE SEEING." With this precept in mind, a visitor may find both obvious and hidden angels in Pasadena's historic Church of the Angels.

The church, completed in 1889, is on land once belonging to Jose Maria Verdugo's Rancho San Rafael. In 1883 an Englishman of Scottish descent, Alexander Campbell-Johnston, purchased about 2000 acres of the rancho on the west side of the Arroyo Seco. Leaving three of his sons to tend the property, he and his wife returned to England.

The area contained fields of barley, hay and oats, vineyards, pasture for goats and sheep, and occasionally a field of red peppers or tomatoes. Ranching continued there until about 1920. Campbell-Johnston referred to his property as Annandale, after his ancestral home in Annandale, Scotland. But Campbell-Johnston died in 1888 while visiting his ranch, and his wife determined to build a church there in his memory.

At that time, the town of Pasadena was hard to reach across the Arroyo Seco, as the large bridges had not yet crossed that natural barrier. So Mrs. Campbell-Johnston situated her church near the settlement of Garvanza, today's Highland Park. (The City of Los Angeles has recently restored the name of Garvanza to the neighborhood.)

Mrs. Campbell-Johnston commissioned plans by the prominent English architect, Arthur Edmund Street. Another Englishman then living in Los Angeles, Ernest A. Coxhead, adapted them to the hilly topography of the site. Construction took just six months in 1889, from Easter Eve to the Feast of St. Michael and All Angels (April to September).

The exterior is of honey-colored sandstone quarried in the San Fernando Valley; the interior is of pressed brick. The design was loosely based on Holmbury St. Mary's Church, near Dorking, Surrey, England. A stone tower rises on the south side of the church, bearing a large Seth Thomas clock installed in 1889. A small arched cloister shelters the entrance, and a porte-cochere with curvy roof extends to the south.

Now about those angels: you'll see one outside as a sculpture in a garden circle. This is a memorial to Mrs. Campbell-Johnston and it's a sundial, with the angel's shadow pointing across the grass to the proper hour.

Indoors, you'll see angels in the large stained glass window (executed in London) and the carved lectern with St. Michael Archangel (from a Belgian carving school.). A porcelain and glass mosaic shows the Archangel Gabriel, looking rather Byzantine—a memorial to three Campbell-Johnston children who died young. Look too for the outlines of angels and their wings, in the woodwork.

The earthquake of 1971 damaged the tower, which had to be shortened. But after the church's centennial in 1989, the height was restored and the whole building strengthened. Today the surrounding hills have been covered with homes, but the church still retains four acres, where it glows in the sunlight between winter storms.

How to get there: The Church of the Angels is at 1100 Avenue 64. From the 110 Freeway, exit at York Ave. and drive west. Turn right on Avenue 64. Call (323) 255-3878.

El Molino Viejo (The Old Mill)
◇ *San Marino* ◇

VISITING SAN MARINO'S El Molino Viejo you will find multi-level gardens with native plantings, mossy patios, and ramadas (shade shelters), so pleasing on a sunny day it may be difficult to go inside.

The Mill itself was built around 1816 as a grist mill for the Mission San Gabriel, about two miles southeast. Like many of our oldest landmarks, it is kept accessible by devoted volunteer effort. The gardens are the continuing work of the Diggers Garden Club, and the California Art Club now has its gallery in the Mill.

Inside the brick wall of the grounds are beds of rosemary, lavender, and native coral bells. An oval ramada is covered with yellow Lady Banks roses. Olives underfoot and fragrant citrus trees recall early California plantings.

The scallop shell-shaped courtyard boasts another Lady Banks growing along the east wall of the Mill. This variety blooms in March, a month earlier than many other roses. Large pomegranate trees curve around the courtyard and quiet fountain, and blue-flowering

native lilac grows in beds edged with roof tiles. Another oval arbor, to the northwest, lifts an ancient grapevine. Green moss literally glows on old paving stones.

The two-story Mill was built of oven-baked adobe brick and volcanic tuff, its walls three to five feet thick, its roof tiled. The upper level once contained the grinding room, where heavy stones ground grain from the Mission lands, and also the granary for storage.

Down a narrow stairway is the wheel chamber with its low vaulted ceiling. Here visitors may see an operating model of the grist mill and illustrations of the building's ownership over the years.

Such a long history is bound to be complex. Padre Jose Maria de Zalvidea, the able administrator of the San Gabriel Mission, designed and built the Mill with Indian labor. The site was chosen for streams threading down nearby canyons and ending in Wilson Lake—which is now San Marino's Lacy Park.

Following secularization of the missions (about 1833), the Mill was used as a residence for a hundred years. Among its owners were Henry Huntington and his family. The last private owner, James Brehm, willed El Molino Viejo to the City of San Marino in 1962. Now the City cooperates with the non-profit Old Mill Foundation to operate and maintain the historic building.

This is one of the most mellow spots you can visit in the San Gabriel Valley. The structure is in good repair, showing its age clearly but with grace. One staff member at the Mill recalls several earthquakes she experienced there. The mysterious booming of one turned out to be millstones rolling around on the lower level, but the historic building remained solid.

With its natural setting and romantic past, you will find a slice of California history as you step into the patio of the Old Mill.

How to get there: El Molino Viejo is at 1120 Old Mill Road. From the 210 Freeway, drive south on Lake Avenue, which becomes Oak Knoll Avenue. Turn left on Old Mill Road. Call: (626) 449-5458.

Lacy Park as Wilson Lake
✧ *San Marino* ✧

MISSION LAKE, Kewen Lake, Wilson's Lake—these were all one and the same, different names for a historic natural feature under a curving brow of hills.

"One of the fairy spots to be met with so often in California," wrote Alfred Robinson, a traveler visiting the San Gabriel Mission lands in 1828. "A beautiful lake…lies calm and unruffled in front, and all around fresh streams are gushing from the earth and scattering their waters in every direction." Today this same spot, its 12 acre lawn shaped like a drop of water, is Lacy Park in San Marino.

Consider the terrain as you visualize this now-gone lake. Lacy Park is bordered on the north and northwest by sharply rising hills. West of the park still stands the Old Mill, built by Mission fathers around 1816 near a canyon stream. Natural springs occurred all along the hillsides. The water table was high in the days of sparse population.

A sizable lake gathered in the natural hollow, bordered by rushy thickets. On some old maps it is named for Col. Edward Kewen, California's first attorney general, who bought the Old Mill and the west side of the lake in 1859. It was also called Wilson's Lake, for Benjamin D. Wilson (Don Benito) who acquired his Lake Vineyard property just to the east in the early 1850's.

By 1900 the lake was a boggy swimming hole for local children, including young George Patton, the future general, who recalled that a raccoon outwitted hunting dogs by swimming to a floating stump. But irrigation of surrounding orchards and vineyards, followed by housing development, finally reduced the lake to mud. In 1923 the owner, Robert Frick, wished to sell off the land into small lots. The City of San Marino, with a $80,000 bond issue and a $10,000 contribution from Henry Huntington, acquired the property for "a civic gathering place" to be called City Park.

William Hertrich, superintendent of the Huntington estate, and Armin Thurnher, who had studied horticulture with Hertrich in Germany, drew up the park plans. There would be a botanical garden of rare trees and shrubs, many donated by Huntington. Thurnher, first superintendent of the park (1926), laughed that he had inherited a big puddle with hundreds of willow trees filled with millions of ants.

Basements for Caltech buildings in Pasadena were being excavated at the time, and dump trucks brought in fill dirt for days, finally leveling the old lakebed. Some 90,000 cubic yards of soil came in from the diggings. Then the present broad lawn was planted, along with 2,000 trees and shrubs. The rose arbor with 175 bushes was added in 1930.

Strolling in the grassy acres today, you can easily imagine their watery past. In one last name change, the spot was called Lacy Park, after Richard Lacy, mayor of San Marino at the park's inception and a City Council member for 29 years.

How to get there: From the 210 Freeway, exit at Lake Ave., drive south, turn left on Arden Rd., right on Oak Grove St., right on Virginia Rd. to the park entrance. For information, call (626) 300-0700.

La Presa Dam

◇ *San Marino* ◇

THE EARLY WATERWORKS of Southern California can still be traced today, under our modern cities. One very old "survivor", the La Presa dam just east of San Marino, was built in 1821 and is still with us.

Artesian springs created marshy ponds long ago, in this site just north of today's Huntington Drive. The native Americans favored the spot for its abundant plant and animal life. Then in 1771 Franciscan friars established the Mission San Gabriel Archangel to the south. Their first church, too close to the San Gabriel River, was

flooded out and replaced by the mission still standing today, where it was built in 1775.

Soon the mission settlement included acres of corn and wheat, olives and fruit trees, with pasture for great herds of cattle. Water was critical to all this life. The padres looked north to the hills along the Raymond Fault, where streams flowed down canyons or rose in springs.

The Indian workmen constructed

"zanjas", or irrigation ditches, across the mission lands. In 1816, they built a water-powered grist mill known today as El Molino Viejo or the Old Mill, a historic landmark open to visitors in San Marino.

But by 1821 Padre Jose Maria Zalvidea decided to replace this "old mill" with a new one, closer to the mission and more efficient. For this task, he chose Joseph Chapman, a New Englander and ship builder.

A series of adventures had brought Chapman first to Hawaii, then to Monterey where he either was captured or surrendered to the Californians. But his skills soon made him valuable, and he worked freely on projects: mills at several missions, the Plaza Church at Los Angeles, and the building of sailing ships.

Chapman's new grist mill was built just south of the mission and little of it survives today. To impound water for the mill, his workmen created a stone and mortar dam across a "cienega" or marshy place long known to the Indians. Stones were carefully fitted, while limestone from the Puente Hills and seashells were burned into lime for the mortar.

The dam, about ten feet high and 225 feet long, was finished with a coating of mortar in which palm prints of the workmen can be seen to this day. The La Presa dam was then linked to Chapman's mill by an irrigation canal lined with clay tiles (no trace of this is known today).

In 1833 the California missions were secularized and a series of other owners held title to the land with the La Presa dam: the Scotsman Hugo Reid, then Henry Dalton, then Leonard Rose on his famed Sunny Slope Ranch. Today the old dam, no longer in use but carefully preserved, is on property owned by the Sunny Slope Water Co.—itself a historic water enterprise founded in 1895.

How to get there: To see the dam, visit a historic marker at approximately 1035 La Presa Ave. From the 210 Freeway, exit at San Gabriel Blvd.and drive south; turn left on Huntington Drive and left on La Presa.

E. Waldo Ward Ranch
✧ *Sierra Madre* ✧

IMAGINE AN OASIS of early Southern California citrus culture, set in a modern-day town. Its turn-of-the-century buildings are edged with orange, kumquat and tangerine trees. This is the E. Waldo Ward Ranch of Sierra Madre.

The foothill settlement of Sierra Madre began with ranches and groves, but today all are gone, except for the property purchased in 1891 by E. Waldo Ward of Elizabeth, New Jersey. Like many nineteenth-century Southern Californians, Ward had come out to recover his health. Arriving in Lamanda Park (now East Pasadena) in 1887, he explored Sierra Madre on horseback and then purchased 10 acres of land from town founer Nathaniel Carter. Later he added 20 acres more.

Soon Ward married and settled on his ranch in a new three-story

house, built of redwood in 1903 and still occupied by his descendents. Behind the house on Highland Avenue, a large red barn had been completed in 1902. Its tower was originally used to store the weekly delivery of water. In the barn today is a small museum with implements from the past and the beautiful orange crate labels used to ship the ranch-grown fruit. (This is a most informal museum; simply, the items once used and needed in that barn are still there.)

E. Waldo Ward, Sr. traveled for many years as a salesman of imported foods. But he long wished to grow the bittersweet oranges used for elegant English marmalade. Finally he acquired two Seville orange trees, the first of their kind in America. As grafting stock, the two produced a grove of over 600 trees. In 1918, pleased with his recipe experiments, Ward established the preserving business still thriving on his ranch.

Ward's marmalade was found on railroad dining cars for years on America's trains, and his products served a wide market when World War I cut off food imports from abroad.

In time, Ward's son E. Waldo Jr, took over the business, which is now run by his son Richard and Richard's son Jeff, the third and fourth generations of Wards. Subdivisions of the growing town have reduced the ranch to just a few acres, but a visitor walking down the dirt road past the tangerine trees today steps into the old years. Across from the red barn, the original cooking and packing facility is still in use, employing modern methods. Additional family acres in Azusa provide some of the fruit.

Great-grandfather's standards are still kept. While the large-scale companies use the residue of juice oranges for their marmalade, Ward uses only fresh whole fruit. The current list shows 15 different marmalades, 19 jellies, and 23 kinds of preserves and jams, in addition to condiments and hand-packed Spanish olives. Some are made up for private labels, or put into gift packages.

Whether your taste is for history or the classic bittersweet marmalade, you'll find the Ward Ranch a refreshing oasis.

How to get there: The ranch is at 273 E. Highland Ave., Sierra Madre. From the 210 Freeway, drive north on Baldwin Ave. to Highland Ave., then turn right. Call (626) 355-1218.

Richardson House & Lizzie's Trail Inn
✧ *Sierra Madre* ✧

BEFORE THERE WAS A TOWN, there was a trail. In 1864, Benjamin D. Wilson (known as Don Benito), who had arrived in California 23 years earlier from Tennessee, began work on a trail to Wilson's Peak from present-day Sierra Madre.

Wilson sought timber from the mountain groves of incense cedar and pine, to make fence posts and shingles for the towns below. His trail followed Little Santa Anita Canyon about seven miles to the peak now named for him.

At the foot of the trail today are two buildings of uncertain age but undoubted charm, their history intertwined with the earliest days of Sierra Madre.

Nathanial C. Carter, a native of Massachusetts, founded the town in 1881 by buying property from E. J. (Lucky) Baldwin, the Southern Pacific Railroad, and Levi Richardson—a total of 1103 acres. Soon the town was divided into twenty and forty acre ranches, later subdivided into smaller parcels.

Levi Richardson's father, John, had arrived in the area in the 1860's and at some point built two cabins on his land. One was the present Richardson House, a four-room cottage with lean-to kitchen. Like many early foothill residents, the Richardsons raised bees for honey.

Later, stables for the horses and mules used on the Mt. Wilson Trail stood just east of the house. They remained until 1961. The City of Sierra Madre acquired the house in 1971 and created Mt. Wilson Trail Park, a grassy playground, where the barns and pack animals had been.

The little structure just to the north, probably dating from the 1880s, was Lizzie's Trail Inn. Providing food and supplies, it was operated by Lizzie McElwain (who died in 1939) and it became locally famous for fried chicken and baked beans.

Like many old buildings of our region, these have traveled. Probably both were moved to their present spots (Lizzie's from the other side of the trail when the City needed that land for a reservoir). The Richardson house was occupied by the restaurant keepers and/or the stable operators over the years.

Today Lizzie's is "sitting tight" under a spacious coast live oak, in the process of restoration. The Richardson House has fresh paint and a native-plant garden with the illusion of a mountain stream.

Volunteers have put in many hours on the two, which are occasionally open to visitors. In the Richardson House, the Sierra Madre Historical Society presents exhibits of town and mountain history. Contact that Society for information on open dates and special events involving the two buildings.

Across the road is a marker honoring Ambrose Zaro (1900-1990) for his lifelong dedication to maintaining the Mt. Wilson Trail. Above this historic intersection, Don Benito's footpath climbs the canyon, as it has for 130 years.

How to get there: The Richardson House is at 167 Mira Monte Ave. From the 210 Freeway, drive north on Baldwin Ave., then right two blocks on Mira Monte. Contact the Sierra Madre Historical Society via the Sierra Madre Public Library at (626) 355-7186.

Church of the Ascension

✧ *Sierra Madre* ✧

THE SURVIVAL OF Sierra Madre's Episcopal Church of the Ascension, for more than 100 years, could be called providential. The Biblical forces of wind, fire and earthquake have not prevailed as the church carries on into its second century.

Fanny Hawks and her mother, arriving from Wisconsin in the 1880's, were determined to found an Episcopal church in the village of Sierra Madre. The only other Protestant church in the San Gabriel Valley was five miles away, along dubious roads if any (the Church of Our Saviour in San Gabriel, which is also still flourishing.)

Fanny gave an acre of her land, and a little frame church went up on Baldwin Avenue in 1885. Only two years later, a Santa Ana wind, violent in the treeless landscape, blew it down.

Ernest Coxhead, an English architect, designed the new building after the stone churches of his native Sussex. The parishioners themselves, some former shipbuilders, did the work. They hauled boulders from nearby Little Santa Anita Canyon and made a stone foun-

dation. A square bell tower and half-timbering completed the English look. The church was neat and snug as a ship in port, finished in 1888.

The sanctuary still contains some very old stained glass. The windows around the altar and in the south transept were shipped around the Horn. One of the Church's bells was rescued from an English vessel which had been wrecked on the Oregon coast. The other, made in Troy, New York, was a Christmas gift from the parish children in 1898. These bells still ring each Sunday.

In 1971, the Sylmar earthquake seriously weakened the aging church. The parish discussed demolition and starting over with a new building. Then preservation architect Raymond Girvigian inspired and supervised the needed work. After this careful recovery, Church historian Catherine Turney quoted Shakespeare: "Out of this nettle, danger, we pluck this flower, safety."

Danger struck even more forcefully in 1991, with the Sierra Madre earthquake. Stones of the tower separated. "We could see daylight through them," recalls the present Rector, Rev. Michael Bamberger. He himself, as a Sierra Madre volunteer fireman, "yellow-tagged" the church to show it was unsafe to enter.

The 1971 repairs had strengthened the tower for the 1991 shock. In a nine-month project, the tower was "stitched" together by drilling diagonal holes through the thick stone walls and lacing them with steel. Grout forced in under pressure then refilled the cracks from the inside. The wrecking ball had been outwitted once again.

When you visit, notice the varied stonework, the traditionally English lych-gate into the garden, and the curving interior woodwork which resembles the hull of a ship turned over your head ("ship" is the meaning of the "nave" of a church.) Today, the Church of the Ascension is listed on the National Register of Historic Places.

How to get there: From the 210 Freeway, drive north on Baldwin Ave. to the Corner of Laurel Ave. (the church address is 25 Laurel Ave.) Call (626) 355-1133.

Pinney House
◇ *Sierra Madre* ◇

"THE BEST THING IN TOWN," wrote Southern California architectural historian Robert Winter. And it certainly is a sight for sore eyes, the three-story Queen Anne-style Pinney House in Sierra Madre.

The Pinney House still has elbow room worthy of its size. It seems to preside over the neighborhood, as it has since 1887, with its east-facing veranda catching the early morning sun. Behind it rise the gray-green San Gabriel Mountains.

Architects Samuel and Joseph Newsom designed the building for Dr. Elbert Pinney, who had bought land from Sierra Madre's founder Nathaniel Carter. The Newsoms also created the exuberant Carson Mansion in Eureka, California, and the San Dimas Hotel (now known as the San Dimas Mansion).

The Pinney House was first a hotel called the Sierra Vista. It served prospective land buyers and resort visitors. The town's Chamber of Commerce held dinners in the cupola dining room overlooking the

Valley. The 40-acre tract surrounding the building had sold for $50 an acre before the land boom of the 1880's; later, Pinney was able to sell part of the property for $1,000 an acre.

Social events flourished at the hotel. Parties from Los Angeles, Pasadena, and other towns arrived in tally-ho carriages. Some guests stayed over to hike the trail to Mt. Wilson the next day. Records show that Mrs. Sara Collins, owner in 1908, gave dancing lessons to local children in the hotel ballroom. There were tennis courts, and an early Sierra Madre tennis club was formed there. From the top of the 80-foot tower, guests could see the Pacific Ocean.

In the 1920s the building became the Hord Sanitarium for treatment of addictions. Then for a time it was used by patients with asthma and respiratory ailments.

Movie makers have sought out the house over the years, shooting such films as "A Great Man's Lady" with Barbara Stanwyck and "The Seven Little Foys" with Bob Hope in 1954. Hollywood carpenters for the "Foys" added some of the gingerbread woodwork you see now.

The Pinney House has even been a birthday present. In 1963 Sierra Madrean Hugh Warden bought it and gave it to his wife Veronica, who loved things Victorian. In 1988 at the age of 101 years the house was fully restored, strengthening foundations, walls, and woodwork.

Today the Pinney House holds nine apartments in about 10,000 square feet of living space. Its 3,000 square foot attic forms a third floor apartment. Paint sampling revealed that dark green was the original exterior color, but restorers kept the more modern creamy white. A swans-neck pediment accents the arching doorway. The complicated facade has many features to notice, and the open space lets us take in the architecture of a less-crowded time.

A walk in this pleasant neighborhood will be satisfying; then consider lunch or coffee in Sierra Madre's village downtown, at the corner of Baldwin and Sierra Madre Blvd.

How to get there: The Pinney House is at 225 N. Lima St. From the 210 Freeway, exit at Baldwin Ave., drive north, turn left on Sierra Madre Blvd. and right on Lima. Contact the Sierra Madre Historical Society via the city's Public Library, at (626) 355-7186.

Rialto Theater
◇ *South Pasadena* ◇

IT WAS OCTOBER OF 1925—a grand opening with search-lights swirling in the night sky, an organist at the mighty Wurlitzer, and a fantasy interior ready to present the illusions of the stage. (Imagine the automobiles that would have been at the scene). No, this was not Hollywood, but the Rialto Theater in South Pasadena.

The Rialto is one of the finest and least changed works of noted theater designer L.A. Smith, who died in 1926 in the prime of his career. Among his neighborhood movie palaces are the Brooklyn Theater in East Los Angeles, the Highland Theater in Highland Park, the Beverly Hills Theater (now a bank), and the Ritz and Uptown, now demolished.

On that opening night the Rialto orchestra accompanied the world premiere of the film "What Happened to Jones?" Five vaudeville acts from the Fanchon and Marco circuit joined the bill, including trapeze artists the Aerial La Valles, Norma Gregg in "an original novelty," and a Dance Carnival number.

The Rialto was outfitted with 10 dressing rooms, a scenery loft, a green room, a deep stage and orchestra pit, so it could accommodate all the entertainment forms of the day. Admission was 30 cents that night; 40 cents for the loge.

The architectural style has been called Spanish Baroque, though reporters of the 1920s described it as Moorish, East Indian, and even Egyptian in touches. The auditorium is decked out with stencilling, plaster ornaments, harpies, gargoyles, fancy fixtures and the organ screen. Above the proscenium arch, a devilish face fixes the audience with lighted red eyes. "A benevolent gargoyle, not threatening," said a one-time manager of the theater. Note too the Batchelder tile drinking fountain in the lobby, with its picture tiles.

For a decade the Rialto served as the try-out stage for new vaudeville talent. For a while a three-act play was offered prior to the feature film twice a week. Then in the late 1930s a fire damaged the backstage area. Neither vaudeville nor live theater ever returned.

Depression times brought marketing ingenuity. Dish Night, for example, provided for each patron a piece of the colored glassware now prized as Depression glass. Keno was played on Bank Night (grand prize was $1.00).

The Rialto has been open without interruption for 75 years. In the 1970's and 1980's concerts were offered by such famed organists as George Wright and Gaylord B. Carter. When redevelopment called for demolition of the theater in 1977, citizens rallied to save the building. It was added to the National Register of Historic Places in 1978.

The Rialto's organ has been removed and sold, but its live stage facilities, including dressing and rehearsal rooms, are all still intact— though unused for many years. As one of the last big theaters, the Rialto seats about 1100, specializing in independent art films, foreign and historic films. Tri-plexes and multi-plexes we may have aplenty, but there is only one Rialto Theater of South Pasadena.

How to get there: From the 210 or the 110 Freeways, drive south on Fair Oaks Ave. to the Rialto, at 1023 Fair Oaks. Call: (626) 799-9567.

Meridian Iron Works

◇ *South Pasadena* ◇

1887 WAS A FINE YEAR in Southern California. The "Boom of the Eighties" was bringing a stream of people into the area, and the economy was strong. Real estate was a flourishing trade. New towns were popping up as fast as someone could draw a plan. (Did you notice how many San Gabriel Valley towns had their centennials during the 1980s?)

Among the new buildings, a little redwood grocery store opened that year in South Pasadena, a year before the city was incorporated. Early photographs show store proprietor Aaron McReynolds at his counter, surrounded by tins and barrels of his goods, with dried herbs hanging from the ceiling.

Today, that building is known as the Meridian Iron Works, owned by the City of South Pasadena as its history museum. How many

lives can such a simple little structure have? Records show this one has been a ticket office, telegraph station, chapel, bicycle shop, and (within living memory) an iron foundry.

With the Santa Fe Railroad running just a few feet away, the building was handy for ticket sales, for a time.

In the 1930s the Nazarene congregation met there while constructing its own church nearby.

In the earliest years of our communities, buildings like this one were so simple, so generic, that they could fill whatever needs were at hand. As the city grew and changed, some new use would always come up and the little structure lived on. Few such examples survive today, so the Meridian Iron Works is an intriguing place to visit and think about.

Step inside the historical museum to see the original context of the building. It was built in the first town center, today called the Historic Business District along Mission Street. The museum has walking tour leaflets for exploring the neighborhood. Across Meridian from the museum is the picturesque stone watering trough and wayside station, a gift to the city in 1907 from the Women's Improvement Association, to benefit horsemen riding into Los Angeles.

Museum exhibits show the two Raymond Hotels which once attracted Eastern gentry to South Pasadena as a winter haven. There's a replica of the town's Santa Fe Depot, torn down in 1954, and advertising notices of the Mt. Lowe Railway ("the railroad in the sky" of our local San Gabriel Mountains.)

The Cawston Ostrich Farm is well illustrated here, with photographs, sample plumes, and a giant egg. This thriving South Pasadena business, which was just a few miles to the west, drew thousands of visitors between 1896 and the 1930's. The museum's three-seater ostrich carousel-animal (1910) is probably one of a kind.

Around the museum are the little odds and ends of our past, which were the stuff of life a few generations ago. You'll see a length of wooden water pipe; a hutch with the old soaps and sundries needed everyday; a sharpening wheel to keep orchard tools working and life going on.

How to get there: The Meridian Iron Works is at 913 Meridian Ave. From the 210 Freeway, exit at Fair Oaks Ave. and drive south. Turn right on Mission Ave. and left on Meridian. Call (626) 799-9089.

South Pasadena Public Library

◇ *South Pasadena* ◇

SOMETIMES A HISTORIC BUILDING evolves like an onion, with additions around its original heart like layers. The South Pasadena Public Library is such a historical onion, and at its center is the city's Carnegie Library of 1908.

South Pasadena established its public library, as an institution, in one room of a local building in 1895. That was the same year the first Raymond Hotel burned down, and the city was first linked to Pasadena and Los Angeles by an electric interurban railway. Two years later, a catalog showed 720 books in the library's collection.

Soon the library needed more space, and South Pasadenans turned to the philanthropic Andrew Carnegie, Scottish-born industrialist and steel magnate. Carnegie eventually gave about $350 million of his fortune to various causes—beginning with New York's Carnegie Hall in 1892 and later constructing over 2,800 public libraries.

In 1906 Carnegie replied with $10,000 for a library in South Pasadena, if the city furnished the site and at least $1,000 in annual main-

tenance. Architect Norman Foote Marsh designed a six-room building with a domed skylight and pairs of columns across the front. This library, the heart of the "onion", was praised by Carnegie when he visited it in 1910. He even found one of his own books on its shelves.

But still more space was needed by 1930. Marsh and his partners, D. D. Smith and Herbert J. Powell, remodeled and expanded the building to nearly double its size (first it was moved from the corner of its park-like block to the center.)

The exterior was redesigned with Spanish and Italian influence. The elaborate doorway, now the entrance to the Community Room, faced north. A carved frieze around the top of the exterior walls carries ten author names suitable for a "California reading list," including John Muir, Richard Henry Dana, Luther Burbank, Bret Harte, Mary Austin, and Joaquin Miller.

But libraries must ever be growing, and in 1981 work began on still another addition. This time the new main entrance would face south, to Oxley Street. Herbert Powell, who had worked on the 1930 "layer", served as consultant and his partner Howard Morgridge was now the principal architect.

85,000 books were moved into storage, and the new section was built with simple lines. A small colonnade leads to an entrance courtyard. The library's oak tables and chairs, most dating back to 1930 and some to 1908, were refinished. The oak of the old circulation desk was transformed into exhibit cases. A little book sales room created upstairs is intriguing.

With its present 24,500 square feet of space, the library is about six times the size of the original Carnegie building. For the moment, South Pasadena's "historical onion," filled with books and readers, is complete.

How to get there: The Library is at 1100 Oxley St. From the 110 Freeway, exit at Fair Oaks Ave. and drive south; turn right on Oxley St. Call (626) 403-7333.

Oaklawn Waiting Station & Bridge
✧ *South Pasadena* ✧

WHAT WERE FOLKS waiting for, at the rugged stone waiting station still standing on Fair Oaks Avenue in South Pasadena?

Years ago, they were waiting for the Pacific Electric trolleys, the Pasadena Short Line to be exact, which opened in 1902 and ran beside Raymond Hill with its famed hotel, the Raymond. Henry Huntington's Big Red Cars traveled down sparsely settled Fair Oaks past open fields and on to Los Angeles.

Subdivisions sprang up convenient to the Short Line, including Oaklawn—advertised as a parklike settlement favored for its oaks and orange trees. The tract was plotted out in 1905, with entrance portals on Columbia Street designed by Charles and Henry Greene.

At the south end of Oaklawn Avenue the Greenes designed their first and only bridge, to span a railway and cycleway, then connect with Fair Oaks Avenue. The reinforced concrete structure used new methods developed by Michael de Palo, an engineer who had just

created a long arch-bridge at Playa del Rey. But the Oaklawn bridge proved difficult, and initial cracks caused alarm. Finally with extra support somewhat spoiling the design, the bridge stood firm: a 340-foot span in five long simple arches.

At the east end of the bridge stands the waiting station with its giant boulders. This too is the Greenes' design, built in 1906. A more solid, even ponderous, building is hard to imagine. The tile roof is strongly horizontal, upheld by heavy timbers. Roof beams project two feet beyond the tiles. A strong sense of permanence and of shelter is in the massive stones.

South Pasadena was developing rapidly in those years. In 1907 the high school opened with 65 students, and a volunteer fire department was authorized. The first home delivery of mail followed the next year. And in 1909 the city's first automobile showroom opened. No one could have known how its descendents would someday bring an end to the red trolleys at the Oaklawn waiting station.

The Greene brothers continued their distinctive work, experimenting with the hefty stonework and sheltering eaves. Two of their most famous homes soon followed: Pasadena's Blacker House in 1907, and the Gamble House in 1908. But no more bridges.

Today, the Oaklawn bridge is for pedestrians only, as traffic on Fair Oaks is too busy to admit access from the little span. The Oaklawn tract is now somewhat isolated and so perhaps as peaceful as it was ninety years ago. A stroll along Oaklawn Avenue is worthwhile to see the variety of architecture, including Craftsman-style houses (none by the Greenes, however.)

The waiting station has been recently restored, and it maintains a forlorn dignity. It is now a Cultural Heritage Landmark of South Pasadena. Although there is nothing to wait for there, at present, its survival suggests that public transportation may someday revive and bring it to life again.

How to get there: The waiting station is at Fair Oaks Avenue and Mound Street. From the 210 Freeway, exit at Fair Oaks and drive south. From the 110 Freeway, exit at Fair Oaks and drive one block north. For information, call (626) 799-9089.

Bells, San Gabriel Mission - San Gabriel California

Alhambra Historical Museum
◇ *Alhambra* ◇

IT WAS RATHER an unusual present, among many things given
to the Alhambra Historical Society. But as the city's "attic" in the
public library threatened to overflow with relics of the past, Dr.
Willard Gayle Thompson, a local physician, gave them his medical
office building. Moved to a city lot in 1987, this present was ready to
become a museum.

Today it's chock full, but in an organized way. Several rooms are
devoted to Alhambra's origins, the town established by B.D. Wilson
(Don Benito) in the 1870's. In the museum's library is a photographic
book of the town's namesake: the gorgeous Alhambra, 14th century
citadel of the Moorish kings of Spain near Granada. You must see
this.

Don't be in a hurry when you come to browse in a museum like
this, or you will miss some choice things. What about Alhambra's
Airport, active from 1930-46, with the Goodyear Blimp tethered there

in a photograph? What about the Alhambra Art Colony, where Norman Rockwell stayed for a time and married an Alhambra girl?

Then there was that unique industry, the Standard Felt Co., which made dozens of slipper styles in five large brick buildings (now replaced by a Target store). The colorful Alfred Dolge founded this company, Alhambra's largest employer in the early 1900's, where the wool felt dried to perfection in "300 days of sunshine a year."

But this museum is not just about Alhambra. It's about the small things of daily life, long ago. Yes, your mother had one just like that, or it was at your grandparents' house—home medicines, or the Little Lulu dish towels that say "wash on Monday, iron on Tuesday, sew on Wednesday..."

The kitchen Hoosier (a free-standing cabinet) claimed "less miles, more smiles". Museum volunteers demonstrate another labor-saving device: the manual vacuum cleaner, pumped by hand to create suction.

But your own attic does not have the World War II bomb shown among memorabilia in the Police and Military Room here.

Be sure you see the collection of phonographs, several by Edison, with their fancy sound trumpets known as "morning glory horns." You can follow in a museum like this the progress of technology and what seemed so great in each new decade.

After all, there is no more need for the Ice Dealers Association, its salesmen looking proud here in a group photo, or that window sign for the homeowner to say whether she would like a 25 or 50 pound block of ice today.

After all the relics, it's refreshing to step outside into the museum's new xeriscape garden, named for long-time Alhambra city councilman Talmage V. Burke. Here are bright colored water-saving plants: lavenders and sages, with fuzzy fountain grass responding to the breeze. A bench in the shade offers a spot to take it all in.

How to get there: The museum is at 1550 W. Alhambra Rd. From the 10 Freeway, exit at Atlantic Ave., drive north to Alhambra Rd. and turn left. Call (626) 300-8845.

Walnut Creek Nature Park
✧ *Baldwin Park* ✧

LOOK AGAIN AT your map showing the southern San Gabriel Valley. You'll see the Rio Hondo and the San Gabriel River, flowing south, nearing each other at the Whittier Narrows Recreation Area. Close by, two creeks still flow into the San Gabriel River from the east, each with its own history of early use: San Jose Creek and, just north of it, Walnut Creek.

Today these waterways are controlled in channels and have lost their wildness. But adjoining one, you'll find a 4.5 acre preserve which quietly maintains native plants and rustic paths. This is the Walnut Creek Nature Park in Baldwin Park.

The creek itself, now the southern boundary of Baldwin Park, is outside the fenced enclosure and seems more related to the warehouse cityscape on the opposite bank (the City of Industry). But in the park, with its mature trees, you'll be unaware that both the 605 and the 10 freeways are just a few blocks away.

Pleasant View was the first name for the town here (about 1878), changed to Vineland in 1887. A public school and Vineland Irrigation District anchored the growing settlement in the 1890s. In 1906,

92

the Pacific Electric Railroad was built along Ramona Boulevard. That same year Elias J. "Lucky" Baldwin agreed the town could use his name and become Baldwin Park. In the '30s and '40s, the area held a mix of poultry ranches, walnut and citrus groves, and sand/gravel companies.

Two early families once lived on the Nature Park site: the McMullans, dairy farmers from 1913-24, and the Dospitals, ranchers from 1924-65. The Baldwin Park School District acquired the land for a future school site, then sold it to the City for a park.

In 1976, work began to create the present wooded setting. Nature centers like those at Whittier Narrows and Eaton Canyon provided models for natural history education. Native plants now grow along winding gravel paths.

A stone building, open on several sides, provides a meeting place. The main space has a hearth and exhibits describing Southern California habitats: chaparral, riparian (streamside), oak woodlands, and others. The unusual building resembles an overturned ship, with its prow in the air. The park also has a rustic playground, an outdoor seating area for small groups, and a "parcourse" for fitness practice. Picnic tables and benches are invitingly scattered in green niches.

Plantings include a grove of pines and a chaparral section with ceanothus and toyon. Alders fringe a natural-looking dry streambed. Native oak, sycamore, and California walnut can be found. Aromatic white sage, once used by the Native Americans, is here. The whole effect is pleasantly wild. This is truly a lost and found surprise, but we must take care of it.

How to get there: The Park is at 701 Frazier St. From the 605 Freeway, exit at Ramona Blvd. and drive east. Turn right on Syracuse Ave., left on Bess Ave., right on Athol Ave., and right on Frazier. For current hours or picnic reservations, call (626) 813-5245.

El Monte Historical Museum
◇ *El Monte* ◇

IT WAS THE YEAR 1937 in El Monte, then a semi-rural settlement between two rivers, the San Gabriel and its branch the Rio Hondo. The walnut industry, once a mainstay, had been in decline for several decades, but the town newspaper—the El Monte Herald—was still advertising small farms of one or two acres, enough to sustain a family.

Employment was scarce in the Depression times. So the town was jubilant at the convergence of Federal assistance and the generosity of a local citizen. The citizen was John C. Bodger, whose family had come to El Monte in 1916 and bought old walnut orchards to clear for planting flowers. By 1940 they were operating the world's largest wholesale flower seed business, the Bodger Seed Co., with acres of zinnias, asters, and other blooms.

In the mid-1930's Bodger gave the city a block of his land along Tyler Avenue for a new civic center. Through efforts of Congressman Jerry Voorhis, the Works Progress Administration (WPA) of

the Federal government agreed to put up the buildings: a new library and a community center with auditorium and city offices.

Artisans for the Spanish-style buildings were hired from all the construction trades. The architect was Richard C. Farrell. Hand-hewn beams show the craftsmanship and the unhurried work. The library was finished first, and a branch of the Los Angeles County Library moved in. There was space for 15,000 volumes, and reading rooms for adults and children.

The municipal center next door opened soon after, with ceremonies including a festive ball, vaudeville acts, and dedication by Congressman Voorhis of a plaque, which reads: "Erected by the Works Progress Administration as a work relief project which gave work to 100 men for a period of 2 years."

The dedication was also noted to be the 25th anniversary of the city's incorporation and the 85th anniversary of the founding of the community.

Today these buildings are as handsome as ever, facing a city park across the street also on land donated by the Bodger Seed Co. In 1967 the library was moved to another site and its building became the El Monte Historical Museum.

In 1984 an addition was made to the museum building, the wing to the south. When you visit, look for the six large paintings of Native American scenes, high on the walls. These also go back to the 1930's, when they were created by the Federal Art Project.

In the basement of this building is a 40-year run of the town's newspaper, the El Monte Herald, rescued from near destruction by museum historian Fred Love. With this valuable record and the wide-ranging exhibits, you can learn more about how acres of flowers became a city center. No true history-seeker should miss this museum, one of our best.

How to get there: The museum is at 3150 Tyler Ave. From the 10 Freeway, exit at Santa Anita Ave. and drive south. Turn left on Garvey and left on Tyler. Call (626) 444-3813.

El Monte Rurban Homesteads
✧ *El Monte* ✧

THE GOODYEAR BLIMP and a team of elephants helped in this project. The result was a Southern California village which became a model for the country in Depression times.

In 1933, many citizens of Los Angeles County had annual family income only between $600 and $1,000, even though they were employed. For them, President Franklin Roosevelt devised a program of simple dwellings on small plots which, intensely cultivated, could supply the major food requirements. These were known as subsistence homesteads—also called "rurban" (rural-urban) homes.

After surveying the San Gabriel Valley in the Goodyear Blimp, Federal officials chose a part of El Monte for the project. The fertile land between the San Gabriel River and the Rio Hondo had been covered by some 5,000 acres of walnut groves which were dying out. Elephants from the nearby Barnes Circus pulled out the walnut stumps to clear the site.

The plan called for a colony of 100 small houses, each on about 3/4 acre of land. Fruit trees and chicken houses would combine with vegetable plots, space for animals, and arbors. There would be a school and a community building, with a common kitchen for canning .

Joseph Reston, a local architect, designed the 3, 4, 5, and 6 room houses. Their style was "a fusion of early Californian and New England Colonial." Some of the old walnut trees remained. Finished in 1935, the tract became a model for 60 similar homestead projects around the United States. Later the Secretary of Agriculture pronounced the El Monte project the most successful in the country, and by far the most beautiful in development.

The site plan was two rectangles, joined by a connecting road called "The Wye." About 30,000 applications were received and the homesteaders were selected with care. "Folks will be raising chickens, domestic animals, and children, and must be tolerant of the misbehavior of all of these," said the official literature.

"El Monteans are interested in your adventure in rurban living under the sponsorship of the national government, and look upon you as modern pioneers," said an editorial of welcome in the *El Monte Herald*, in 1935.

The next year, the government reported that 90% of the homesteaders were producing all of their vegetable requirements. Rurban life classes were offered, to teach self-sufficiency on the small plots. The settlers, who were required to have some income, took out 20 year loans with monthly payments of about $21. To prevent speculation, residents were on trial for one year and could not take title for five years.

Today, some homes from this idealistic experiment can still be seen, although the farming land has mostly been subdivided. Boundaries of the original project are Lower Azusa Road, Peck Road, Hemlock Street, and the San Gabriel River. The social history of these times is fascinating and can be explored at the well-organized archives of the El Monte Historical Museum.

How to get there: The Museum is at 3100 No. Tyler Ave. From the 10 Freeway, exit at Santa Anita Ave., drive south, turn left on Garvey Ave. and left on Tyler. Call (626) 444-3813.

Whittier Narrows

✧ El Monte ✧

THIS IS A TALE of two rivers—although they are actually two strands of one ever-changing and temperamental stream, the San Gabriel River.

Life-giving and unpredictable for centuries, the river has shifted its course many times. But geography has always drawn its waters close together again at the historic Whittier Narrows.

Today the two rivers, running roughly parallel for a while, are known as the San Gabriel River and, west of it, the Rio Hondo. Flowing south from the San Gabriel Mountains, these two streams must pass through a gap several miles wide between the Montebello Hills and the Puente Hills, on their way to the sea. This gap, the Whittier Narrows, is like the drain of the vast bathtub of land that is the San Gabriel Valley.

Earthquakes and floods used to cause countless migrations of the streams. In flood years the San Gabriel would leap its banks and

wash over adjacent land. Then its old river-bed would fill with silt and willow thickets, and the stream would cut new channels. Early settlers in the area found their lands either flooded or stranded by the fickle waters.

A violent earthquake of 1857 opened the channel now east of Whittier Narrows (the present San Gabriel River). Early in this century, floods formed the Rio Hondo (meaning "deep river") as an overflow channel of the San Gabriel River. It branches from the main river just north and east of El Monte, flowing southwest and running west of its mother river through the Whittier Narrows. The two blend briefly in the wetlands of the Narrows. Then the Rio Hondo veers west to flow into the Los Angeles River.

Today these rivers wander no more. They are in captivity and keep to their appointed places. But if you live anywhere in the San Gabriel Valley, you are not far from one of the two rivers or their creeks. Most road maps of this area or your Thomas Guide will show you where they are. (We usually look at such maps for streets and freeways. Instead, study yours a while to follow the rivers.)

If you can find a relief map of this area, so much the better. You will plainly see why all that water had to pass through the Whittier Narrows.

A wildlife sanctuary of several hundred acres, with a Nature Center, is now on the west bank of the San Gabriel River. Its four lakes attract migrating birds. The lands belonged to the National Audubon Society from 1939 to 1970, when the County of Los Angeles acquired them.

The Nature Center, with its exhibits and programs, is well worth a visit. The surrounding county park makes a fine family outing for bird walks, picnics, and exploring.

How to get there: The Nature Center is at 1000 N. Durfee Ave. in South El Monte. From the 60 Freeway, exit at Peck Road, drive south, turn right on Durfee Ave. Call (626) 575-5523.

Stanley Ranch Museum
◇ *Garden Grove* ◇

IF YOUR WEEKEND travels take you a bit south, into Orange County, consider stopping at the eclectic outdoor heart of Garden Grove, the Stanley Ranch Museum. (Visiting hours are limited, so call ahead.)

This area was once ranch and pasture land for cattle and sheep—a flat and nearly treeless expanse. In 1874 Alonzo G. Cook bought 160 acres around present-day Garden Grove Blvd. and Euclid, and named

the new settlement Garden Grove. The first school appeared that year, and a post office was authorized in 1877.

A succession of crops followed as the village grew: first wine grapes and raisins, then walnuts and citrus. In 1915, records showed sugar beets as the largest export from Garden Grove, followed by chili peppers, beans, walnuts, pickles, eggs, chickens and eucalyptus oil.

The agricultural days are gone now, but you can visit the 1892 farmhouse of Edward G. Ware, later owned by his daughter Agnes Ware Stanley. Mr. Ware was a horticulturalist who introduced walnut varieties and valencia oranges to this area. When Mrs. Stanley donated the house to the Garden Grove Historical Society in 1970, it came with a two acre citrus grove.

The Society removed the orange trees to make room for historic buildings brought from elsewhere in the city. About twenty structures, of various ages, now surround the Stanley Ranch house: these include a barn, blacksmith shop, barber shop and an early post office. A Victorian cottage and California bungalow have arrived also. Most await restoration and are not yet open to visit.

In a replica of the town's original fire station is a proud 1926 La France fire truck (the first in Garden Grove), polished to a fare-thee-well. A historic garage has been moved to the property too: it was used by Walt Disney in the 1920s as an animation studio.

The house itself is fun to explore, and a docent will take you through. You'll find an Edison cylinder phonograph from about 1900, which works; treadle sewing machines; birds-eye maple furniture in bedrooms upstairs.

In old country houses, the kitchen was the center of things, and this one has loads of intriguing stuff. The ice-box is shaped like an old-fashioned washing machine, the butter churn is horizontal, and a hand-pumped vacuum cleaner must have provided both cleaning and good exercise.

Old ways of ironing, shaving, scrubbing clothes, and "putting up" vegetables are also in evidence. The ingenuity of some of the tools is worth pondering. In the evening, the family could leave domestic chores and enjoy the small 1890 organ, or crank up Mr. Edison's music machine.

How to get there: The Stanley Ranch is at 12174 Euclid Street. From the 605 Freeway, drive east on the 405 Freeway, continue east on the 22 Freeway; exit at Euclid and drive north. Call the Garden Grove Historical Society at (714) 530-8871.

Hsi Lai Temple

⟡ *Hacienda Heights* ⟡

THE TRADITIONS OF this place are ancient, older than anything around the San Gabriel Valley except the mountains and the river.

But the buildings are new, completed in 1988: it's the Hsi Lai Temple in Hacienda Heights, the largest Buddhist monastery and temple in the western hemisphere. Its name means "Coming to the West", to signify the bringing of Buddhism from the East to the Western world. The beliefs of Buddhism began over 2,500 years ago with the enlightenment of Prince Siddhartha under the bodhi or bo tree—a tree

still to be found here and there in Southern California. This symmetrical complex of temples is arranged around a central courtyard. The driveway surrounding the 15-acre site is shaped like a leaf of the bodhi tree.

Visitors are welcome to walk up a series of stairways, passing one large shrine, then the courtyard and gardens, to reach the main shrine. A book shop is tucked in one niche and a little museum in another. At some point, you may pause for tea, then continue exploring.

The visitor must ascend, as the buildings step upward. Beyond the honey colored tile roofs are grassy California hillsides. The sloping courtyard is guarded by traditional creatures: lion-dogs and the dragon-tortoises. Against the sky, the rooflines are edged with bird and animal shapes.

A sharp eye will discover lotuses everywhere, symbolizing purity because the lotus flower is beautiful although it rises from the mud. There are carved lotuses along railings, also engraved and painted ones on beams under the sweeping eaves. Near the main shrine hangs a large bell-shaped gong.

Among the paintings exhibited along the corridors have been several by March Fong Eu, California's Secretary of State. In the museum are Buddhist items from many countries: China, Tibet, Korea, Japan and others. There are sutras (teachings) written on gilded strips of pattra leaves, showing the beauty of handwriting. Miniature rosewood furniture with mother of pearl inlay is eye-catching. Carvings of wood and jade come from many time periods. The collection is small but has its surprises, like the Maitreya Buddha with 100 tiny children climbing over him.

Symbols are abundant here, but the staff will gladly interpret. Guided tours are offered to groups of 10 or more, when scheduled in advance. Individuals may rent cassette recorded self-guided tours. The Hsi Lai Temple has a full schedule of classes, meditations, and celebrations. At the far end of the complex (the tip of the "leaf") are private buildings for the temple's monks and nuns.

Ancient and modern meet here in these hill-cradled buildings. Over 100,000 people visit each year, touching one of the vital cultures now a part of the San Gabriel Valley.

How to get there: The temple is at 3456 South Glenmark Drive. From the 605 Freeway, drive east on the 60 Freeway, exit at Hacienda Blvd., drive south, then left on Glenmark Drive. For information, call (626) 961-9697.

Rowland Dibble Museum
⬥ City of Industry ⬥

IN THE SOUTHERN STRETCHES of the San Gabriel Valley, you'll often meet the names of Rowland and Workman. Who were these early settlers? An excellent way to make their acquaintance is at the small Rowland Dibble Museum in the City of Industry.

The museum is operated by the La Puente Valley Historical Society, an energetic group which has exhibited for 25 years at the Historical Division of the Los Angeles County Fair. Their museum is in a curious round building which was once a ranch water tank used by livestock.

John Rowland and William Workman were Easterners who became business partners in Taos, New Mexico. In 1841, they led a group of forty settlers along the Old Spanish Trail into Southern California, the first wagon train to arrive here from the East.

Together, they obtained title to Rancho La Puente, one of the largest ranches owned by the San Gabriel Mission.

This fine spread of 48,790 acres was bordered on the south by the Puente Hills and on the west by the San Gabriel River. It stretched east to present-day Pomona, north to present-day Covina. Through the center ran the San Jose Creek. The two lifelong friends built adobe homes close to each other, Workman on the north side of the creek and Rowland on the south. Later the ranch was divided equally, Workman owning the western half and Rowland the eastern.

In the museum, you can trace three generations of Rowlands, their ranch life, and the developments on their land. The railroad came to La Puente Valley in 1872, and towns were platted in the land boom of the 1880s. Photographs show, cattle, orchards, and haying on gentle slopes. By 1920, the community had the largest walnut packing house in the world, 300 by 174 feet in size, shown in a photo.

The museum's circular display lends itself to this flow of history. Visitors step along through the years, seeing first the cowboys' tools, then a Victorian bedroom, a turn-of-the-century household, and a kitchen with an Art Eureka wood-burning range and unusual kerosene cookstove.

Workman's home still stands just west of here, in a parklike setting called the Workman and Temple Homestead (Temple was a grandson who built a 1920's home at the same site.)

Rowland's original adobe is gone, but in 1855 he built the first two-story brick house in Southern California. It's here, next to the little museum, although closed to visitors until earthquake repairs can be made. Here the Rowland family lived until John's granddaughter, Lilian Dibble, died in 1959.

Workmans, Temples, and Rowlands still live in the local area, including young John Rowland VII carrying on the family name.

How to get there: The museum is at 16021 Gale Ave. (between Stimson and Hacienda). Drive south on the 605 Freeway, east on the 60 Freeway; exit at Hacienda, drive north, then right on Gale Ave. Call the La Puente Valley Historical Society at (626) 369-7220.

El Campo Santo

Workman and Temple Homestead

✧ City of Industry ✧

OLD CEMETERIES CAN sometimes be read like a book of history. Names and dates abound, showing details of a town's early life. El Campo Santo (the holy ground) in the City of Industry is a private cemetery, one of the oldest in Southern California. It was used only for those who owned the property over the years, and some of their friends.

The story of this place begins in 1841, when John Rowland and William Workman arrived in California. The two friends who had become business partners in Taos, New Mexico, had brought 40 settlers in the first wagon train to arrive here from the East.

Soon they acquired Rancho La Puente, a spread of 48,790 acres formerly owned by the San Gabriel Mission. Through their lands ran the San Jose Creek, in the present City of Industry. The two friends built adobe houses close to each other, Workman on the north side of the stream and Rowland on the south.

Today the site of William Workman's home is preserved in the Workman and Temple Family Homestead Museum. The broad grounds contain a Victorian house built around the original adobe, and a 1920s Spanish Colonial Revival mansion built by Workman's grandson Walter P. Temple. Within the park, to the east, is El Campo Santo.

William Workman had created a one-acre family cemetery and built a Gothic brick chapel, destroyed by fire in 1903. Small private graveyards were common until about 1900, when town planners began to establish public burial grounds. Workman's cemetery had fallen into disuse when the Workman family lost its home and property in 1899. Tenant farmers allowed cattle to graze on the spot. In 1917 grandson Walter Temple (who laid out Temple City in 1922) acquired 75 acres of the original ranch and built a memorial mausoleum to re-establish the old cemetery.

Today El Campo Santo is enclosed by an aging brick wall, possibly of bricks made on the ranch in Workman's time. Two large gingko trees stand like quiet sentinels.

The mausoleum, resembling a Greek temple, has stone veneer outside and marble veneer within. Its 24 crypts hold the remains of family members and also Pio Pico—the last Governor of Mexican California—and his wife. The Picos were first buried in Old Calvary Cemetery near downtown Los Angeles. But city development encroached, so Temple brought their remains to his new mausoleum in the 1920s.

Behind the buildings, a cast iron fence encloses a plot of graves, but their contents remain mostly unknown. A simple obelisk marks the grave of Workman's old comrade: John Rowland, who died in 1873. "Gone home," says the inscription.

This historic site is rich in possibilities, including programs which reveal more than a century of Southern California life.

How to get there: The Homestead is at 15415 East Don Julian Road. From the 605 Freeway, exit at the 60 Freeway and drive east. Exit at Hacienda Blvd. and drive north to Don Julian; turn left. For information, call (626) 968-8492.

Our Lady of Guadalupe Mission
◇ Irwindale ◇

A GROUP OF ARTISTS sits along busy Arrow Highway in Irwindale, intent on their sketching. No matter that gravel trucks roll past, and the rumbles of industry are nearby. Their subject? the little stone church—Our Lady of Guadalupe Mission.

In the late nineteenth century, this was a dry and rocky landscape east of the San Gabriel River. According to a town historian, the Presbyterian Mission Society of New York fostered the first settlement here, to be built by and for the Mexican people. As always in Southern California, water was critical. Cisterns stored rain water in the village, and finally wells provided irrigation. Irwindale was named for a developer of the first wells.

The families were Catholic and they wanted a church. They had neither architect, contractor, nor building fund, but in 1917 they simply began. The young men and children brought rocks and sand from the river, using horses and mules. The adults shaped the fifty by thirty foot building with arched windows and a neatly squared

tower. Women of the community raised funds by selling tamales and holding fiestas with dancing.

After ten months of work, it was time for the first Mass. The altar was a hand-hewn table, and neighboring Azusa parish provided candles and linens.

Over the years the congregation grew, though there was not always a priest in residence and at times the people walked to Azusa for Mass. Many weddings and baptisms were held in the little sanctuary.

But in 1965, a larger Our Lady of Guadalupe church was built in Irwindale. Then the Whittier earthquake of 1987 damaged the handcrafted stone mission. Its future was in doubt, and the property was put up for sale.

"It meant too much to the community to lose it" recalls Teresa Chico, a lifelong Irwindale resident. As a child, she had gone to Mass there with her grandmother, one of the original group which built the church. Irwindale today is an industrial town with a population of only about 1,000. But several families have been there for generations and fondly remember the old mission. Just in time, the city of Irwindale purchased it as a historic landmark.

For the costly earthquake repairs, volunteers came forward once again. One construction company reinforced the church walls, while others donated materials. Volunteers built a low stone wall around the property, patched plaster inside, and painted gold stars in a niche above the altar.

All is quiet now, inside the Guadalupe mission. No regular services are held there, but the sanctuary can be used by arrangement with the city. In the meantime, an active group of descendents and supporters—the Guadalupanas—is watching over the building, which holds so many memories.

How to get there: From the 210 Freeway, exit at Arrow Highway and drive east. The mission is just east of Irwindale Ave. at the corner of Morada St.

San Jose Creek

◇ *La Puente* ◇

IN 1888 the most-needed map in the San Gabriel Valley was not a "Thomas Guide" of streets but a chart of the rivers, creeks, and ditches criss-crossing the land with vital water.

The California State Engineer produced a two volume report that year on *Irrigation in Southern California*. It's a fascinating account of springs and streams, sustaining both the crops and the daily life of early settlers. Today the water is still there but hidden, in our networks of drains, wells, and urban systems.

William Hall, the State Engineer, wrote about San Jose Creek, which he called "a stream of no small importance." This creek arose from springs in the hills south of Pomona, then flowed thirteen miles southwest and into the San Gabriel River (today, near the crossing of the 605 and 60 Freeways).

The source of the creek was a gravel bed beside Elephant Hill near Spadra, an early settlement now part of the city of Pomona. The valley of the creek included some 10,000 acres of "fine arable land,"

with the water supply coming up at intervals in more springs. Along its banks, both agriculture and recreation flourished.

Fourteen major ditches diverted the water to irrigate vineyards, alfalfa, deciduous fruits, corn, and other summer crops. The ditches were from one to six miles in length, some owned by individuals and some by groups.

The oldest ditches operating along San Jose Creek in 1888 were those of John Rowland and William Workman. These pioneers had arrived in Southern California in 1841 and their ditches were dug in 1846-1850. They lived in adobes less than a mile apart beside the San Jose Creek and shared pasture lands.

The State Engineer could also see, in 1888, traces of the irrigating ditches dug by the padres, for these had been San Gabriel Mission lands. The traces were by then 100 years old, as the Mission was founded in 1771 in its original site on the San Gabriel River.

Engineer Hall also recorded the soil types of the area—very fertile, because the unconfined river changed its course frequently, depositing rich silt.

San Jose Creek provided water power for several grist mills, and its deep spots were fishing and swimming holes. The creek was generally 10 to 12 feet below its plain on either side, and its width varied with the seasons.

Photographs from 1895 to 1910 show people picnicking along San Jose Creek, in large groups from the nearby ranches. Shaded by trees, the revellers laze on a summer's day, the men in straw hats and the ladies in long skirts. Many pictures show guitars, violins, even a trumpet.

Today the creek has been straightened and its channel paved. Its path is mostly through the city of Industry, just south of Valley Blvd. (You can trace it in your Thomas Guide.) See a glimpse of what it was, where it flows under Workman Mill Road just north of the 60 Freeway: gravelly shores, some green growth, and perhaps a white egret.

For information: Call the La Puente Valley Historical Society at (626) 369-7220.

Rio San Gabriel Battle Site
◇ *Montebello* ◇

ON BLUFF ROAD in Montebello, at its hectic intersection with Washington Blvd., two cannons point east across the captive waters of the Rio Hondo. The cannons are muzzled, silent companions now for a historic marker. What happened here?

At this point, about 150 years ago, three vigorous characters of early California history led their men into a skirmish. The Battle of the Rio San Gabriel, January 8, 1847, was the last armed battle of the Mexican War, in which California passed into American hands.

On that day, American forces under Commodore Robert E. Stockton, U.S. Navy Commander-in-Chief, and Brig. Gen. Stephen W. Kearny of the U.S. Army, met the Californians led by Gen. Jose Maria Flores. Flores and about 550 men held the high bluff along the Old San Gabriel River, which used to change its course freely during winter floods. Today, the San Gabriel River is channeled about two miles to the east, beyond the city of Pico Rivera, while the stream below the bluff is called the Rio Hondo.

Quicksand in the river bottom made a difficult crossing for the 600 Americans, approaching from the east into artillery fire. But in an hour and a half the victory was theirs, and the Californians retreated toward Los Angeles.

Two days later, Kearny and Stockton entered the plaza of Los Angeles, the city having already surrendered. And on January 13, the War ended with the signing of a treaty at the Cahuenga Adobe (now gone, but preserved as the historic site "Campo de Cahuenga" near Universal Studios in North Hollywood). Mexican rule of California was over, but the co-existence of the two cultures continues to this day.

Flores and his forces had controlled the lands from Santa Barbara to San Diego until the Cahuenga treaty. After the war, he held various commands with the Mexican Army. Kearny later became civil governor of Vera Cruz and Mexico City, but died of a tropical disease only a year after the Rio San Gabriel battle.

Stockton had served in the War of 1812 and even helped with the settlement of Liberia. In July 1846, as American military governor of California, he had declared the region to be U.S. territory, but achieved his goal only by joining forces with Kearny that January day.

To the north of the memorial today, the Montebello Hills and the Whittier Hills face each other to form the Whittier Narrows, about two miles wide. The San Gabriel River and its branch, the Rio Hondo, run parallel at this point, their waters now held in channels and ponds. The San Gabriel flows south, meeting the sea at Long Beach. The Rio Hondo will veer to the west, joining the Los Angeles River at Downey.

The quicksand of this battle site is long gone, and a bridge now spans the crossing. But the bluff is still a vantage point, and the cannons mark a crucial day in California history.

How to get there: From the 605 Freeway, exit at Washington Blvd. and drive west; turn right at Bluff Road. Park with care at this busy spot.

Taylor Ranch House Park
✧ *Montebello* ✧

AN OLD BARN is a rare and intriguing thing to come across in Southern California, especially in the midst of a city. Backed by tall trees, a fine one stands on the south slopes of the Montebello hills, within easy irrigation distance from the San Gabriel River at the Whittier Narrows. What is its history?

The property is now known as Taylor Ranch House Park. According to Harris Newmark, the pioneer merchant and chronicler of Los Angeles history, the land between Whittier and Los Angeles ("this fine domain," he called it) was divided in the 1890s and given water systems under the advice of William Mulholland. The area was named Montebello, and one townsite was briefly known as Newmark.

Soon, Albert Taylor came into the area with the Mormon Battalion, and in 1895 he purchased land to settle down with his family. The barn was built first, then in 1907 a one story clapboard ranch house of five rooms. In 1928, three additions were linked to the house, giving it the rambling quality you'll see today.

The Taylor family seems to have been pioneers in other ways also. Local tradition maintains that oil was pumped directly to the Taylor kitchen from a nearby well, as the Montebello oil fields began to flourish. Also, the first electric light switches in town were there, at the Taylors' home.

In 1976, the barn was restored by the Soroptimist Club of Montebello, and the gabled front porch of the house was moved to the south side to allow for widening of Montebello Boulevard. By then the buildings had a new purpose, as the Taylors had willed their house to their friend, the artist Evelyn White, to live in for the rest of her life.

This enterprising lady brought to the Taylor Ranch the newly formed Southland Art Association, a group of artists who met to share their practice and hold shows. The ranch buildings were becoming an active cultural center. So when some Taylor descendents wanted to sell the property to developers, the City of Montebello purchased it to become a park.

Today, Southland Art continues to meet in the picturesque barn. Newcomers are welcome to inquire about the association. The ranch house is available for rental, to be used by groups for their meetings or to hold community celebrations. Members of the Montebello Historical Society gather there also, enjoying the aura of history about the place.

Whether you picnic in the spacious hilly park, visit the art barn, or contact the historical society, you'll be reaching back to that "fine domain" which bordered a great river, once out in the countryside east of Los Angeles.

How to get there: Taylor Ranch House Park is at 737 N. Montebello Blvd., just north of Lincoln Ave. From the 60 Freeway, exit at Montebello Blvd. and drive south. Call the City's Park and Recreation Dept. at (323) 887-1200.

Sanchez Adobe
✧ *Montebello* ✧

GEOGRAPHY MAY BE destiny when settling in a new land. The western banks of the San Gabriel River attracted two important buildings many years ago, their sites only about a mile apart. One of them was situated too low, too close to the changeable river, and it had to be abandoned after four years.

The other, built high on a bluff overlooking the river, survives to this day. It is the 150-year old Sanchez Adobe in Montebello.

The original wing of the adobe dwelling, the part running north and south, was built about 1845 by Dona Casilda Soto de Lobo and her sons. She had been deeded some 2,300 acres of the Rancho La Merced but eventually could not pay her debts to William Workman of the nearby La Puente ranch. Her family forfeited its property, and half was deeded to Workman's daughter and half to his ranch foreman, Juan Matias Sanchez.

Sanchez occupied the adobe with his wife and five children. Along the river he raised horses for the U.S. Cavalry, selling as many as

116

1,500 head in a year. Widowed at about age 60, he married a bride 16 years old and added three more children to his family. Although E. J. (Lucky) Baldwin eventually took over La Merced, he did allow Sanchez to keep his home until he died in 1885.

By the 1920's the adobe had passed to William Scott and Josephine Scott Crocker, who changed its appearance greatly. Two wings of adobe brick had been added earlier, and the Scotts added a second story. Photographs from that time show incongruous dormer windows and green vines veiling the open porches.

Crocker gave the property to the City of Montebello in 1971, and the old landmark was slowly restored to its original appearance. The Montebello Historical Society placed exhibits showing the early ranch work.

Although closed by damage from the Whittier earthquake of 1987, this historic survivor is again ready for visitors. The great-grandson of Juan Matias Sanchez is sometimes there to talk about the early days. With its fresh-looking shingle roof, the building seems oddly new, but just step inside. Three rooms are restored with timely furnishings.

Outside, look east from the bluff, where the river is now tamed by the Whittier Narrows Dam—a curving earthen dike built by the Army Corps of Engineers in 1952. These were the lands of Sanchez and his horses.

And the other historic building, doomed by river flooding? That was the San Gabriel Mission, built next to the river in 1771 but moved to its present location in the city of San Gabriel in 1775. A marker showing its original site is at the southwest corner of San Gabriel Blvd. and Lincoln Ave. in Montebello.

How to get there: from the 60 Freeway exit at Rosemead Blvd. and drive south. Turn right on San Gabriel Blvd., left on Lincoln Ave. (noting the mission marker), right on La Merced Ave. and right on Adobe Ave. to the end. Call the Montebello Historical Society at (323) 721-3487.

El Encanto

✧ *Monterey Park* ✧

WOULD YOU LIKE to step into the atmosphere of the 1920s, that high-flying decade with so much optimism and style? You can, at Monterey Park's restored El Encanto building and the historic cascades nearby.

In 1928, never imagining the crash that lay just ahead, Peter Snyder opened his Midwick View Estates development in Monterey Park. Snyder was a Greek immigrant with great success in California real estate. At his peak he had five offices, in Pasadena, Long Beach, Alhambra, Fullerton and Los Angeles.

The dapper entrepreneur loved a show, and so he attracted several thousand people to his opening, which featured celebrities, speeches, and Old California dancers. His vision was of beautiful homes around a small park and waterfall, anchored by a meeting place for civic and cultural festivities.

The development's name was derived from the nearby Midwick Country Club, where Will Rogers sometimes played polo. In Snyder's

dream, the area would be a place of enchantment, a rival to Beverly Hills.

By opening day, the re-circulating fountain was complete, with a 240-foot long series of shallow pools cascading down a hillside. Colored lights turned the sparkling waters into a fantasy at night. Lawns and colorful tilework edged the cascades, and a fan-shaped overlook at the top gave a view of Mt. Baldy and other mountains to the East.

At the foot of the cascades stood the Spanish-style sales office for the Estates. A neon sign on the building announced its name: El Encanto (short for Jardin El Encanto: the Enchanted Garden).

By a stroke of historical luck, the cascades, sales building, and original neon sign are in place to this day. The stock market crash drove the project into foreclosure, so houses did not occupy the slopes until many years later. El Encanto careened through many uses, as Oneonta military academy, a wedding chapel, a USO center during World War II, and a private residence. At every change its future was in doubt.

Finally passing into City ownership, the building was renovated and became home to the Monterey Park Chamber of Commerce in March 1995. El Encanto has returned to its original purpose. Once again a community center, it can be rented for meetings and events.

Enjoy the carved hand-tinted woodwork, wrought iron, and colorful tiles, all of the 1920s. There's a musicians' loft, and also a Spanish galleon in stained glass. Mission style furniture suits the period well.

Outside, you can find more Spanish ships in the tile murals. Then walk to the West, up to the overlook to enjoy the mountain view and the setting of Peter Snyder's dream.

How to get there: El Encanto is at 700 El Mercado Ave. From the 10 Freeway, drive south on Atlantic Ave. Just past Harding Ave., the cascades are on right. Left at that point El Portal Place leads one block directly to El Encanto. Telephone (626) 570-9429.

Garvey Ranch Park and
Monterey Park Historical Museum

◇ *Monterey Park* ◇

WHAT'S IN A NAME? Why is this Garvey Ranch Park? Place names often carry the little twists and turns of history.

Our whole Los Angeles basin has a historical layer of ranchos. Most of the lands in our present cities were once granted by Spanish or Mexican authorities to applicants or to soldiers as a reward for military service. More than 50 such titles were issued in the early

19th century. Gradually these ranches were divided and passed into other hands after 1851.

Antonio Maria Lugo held the Monterey Park area in a grant of about 30,000 acres dating from 1810. It was then Rancho San Antonio. The Italian Alessandro Repetto bought a portion in 1866 and raised sheep on the grassy hills. The beginnings of the town came with Richard Garvey, Sr. He bought 5,000 acres here in 1879, becoming the last rancher on these lands.

Garvey's life was incredibly full. He immigrated to Savannah, Georgia from Ireland at the age of 12 and soon was joined by his family. Later he headed west and worked carrying Army mail with pack mules between Los Angeles, Fort Tejon and Fort Mojave. Next he pursued gold mining in Arizona and California, then invested in his ranch lands.

Here he planted orchards and kept horses, building a dam to create a reservoir known as Garvey Lake. He began subdividing the land in 1892, and his settlement was called Ramona Acres (later Monterey Park.) In 1916 town residents voted to incorporate, fending off the hopes of Alhambra and South Pasadena to convert the area into a sewage treatment farm.

Garvey's son, Richard Garvey Jr., built a ranch-style home, and after his death without heirs in 1948 the city created Garvey Ranch Park around it. His house now contains the Monterey Park Historical Museum. The earthen "ridge", with sharp drops on each side, just west of the house, is his father's dam. Today the lake is gone and its hollow holds a baseball diamond. (The large reservoir high above the park belongs to the Metropolitan Water District and was built in 1922).

In the museum you can trace these layers of Monterey Park history. A good introduction is the panels of photographs and newspaper clippings, with wonderful pictures of some Ramona Acres children, the petroleum exploration of the 1920s, even the Monterey Park Glider Club of the 1930s, soaring off the hills. You'll find the museum's brochure in English, Chinese, and Spanish.

Attached to the museum is the Monterey Park Observatory, a building begun by Richard Garvey, Jr. and completed by local astronomers. There the Los Angeles Astronomical Society offers public viewing several evenings a week. You are welcome to observe the night skies and the great beyond.

How to get there: From the 10 Freeway, exit at Garfield Ave. and drive south. Turn left on Graves Ave. and right on Orange Ave., one block to the park. Call the Museum at (626) 307-1267. Call the Los Angeles Astronomical Society at (213) 673-7355

San Gabriel History Walk

✧ San Gabriel ✧

DOROTHY AND TOTO had their Yellow Brick Road. You can pursue a historical walk along a trail of colorful tiles—about 600 of them, made by fourth grade students of San Gabriel schools.

This walk will take you through the San Gabriel Mission District, dedicated in July 1994 as a cluster of landmarks around the 1775 Mission church. You'll see historic markers along the way. And don't dismiss the tiles as just playful children's art. They give some fresh interpretations of history, geography, and the human scene, as you'll see if you read them.

You can begin by picking up a tour brochure at the San Gabriel Historical Museum. Next to it is the Hayes House, built in 1887 for George Bovard, an early Chancellor of USC, and later belonging to one San Gabriel family for nearly 100 years. It has been moved to this site and will be gradually restored.

Your historic ramble will take you to the San Gabriel Civic Auditorium (first known as the Mission Playhouse), its 1927 exterior patterned after Mission San Antonio de Padua. The interior has Indian, Spanish, and Mexican motifs. The Old Grapevine nearby recalls the mission vineyards, which provided cuttings to neighboring ranches.

The Mission itself, with its outside stairway and distinctive bell tower, can be admired from Plaza Park. The City eliminated the section of Mission Drive once running along the south side of the church—now the park and jacaranda trees go right up to the old walls. The park has many plaques, one confirming that Juan Bautista De Anza came this way in 1774, seeking a land route from Sonora, Mexico to California.

From this point, eleven San Gabriel families walked nine miles to the Los Angeles River in 1781, there to establish El Pueblo de la Reina de Los Angeles. Since 1981, this trek has been repeated each year on the anniversary of the original date, done recently by 100 people or more.

Explore the Mission sanctuary, gardens, and cemetery to your heart's content. Then you'll pass the City Hall, on land associated with the pioneering families of Temple, Workman, and Rowland. William Workman and James Rowland organized the first wagon train to reach California over the Santa Fe Trail, arriving in 1841. Walter Temple, who owned this site in 1922, founded Temple City and helped develop other nearby towns.

Arcade shops, once called the Temple Block, offer shade and refreshments across from the Mission and carry on its architectural style. Farther on, a historic general store completes your loop. The children's tiles, with their sparks of humor, have been with you all the way.

How to get there: The Historical Museum and Hayes House are at 546 W. Broadway (626) 308-3223. From the 10 Freeway, exit at Del Mar Ave. and drive north to Broadway, then left to the Museum. The tour brochure is also available at City offices, 606 W. Las Tunas Ave. (626) 308-2800.

Gardens of Mission San Gabriel
◇ *San Gabriel* ◇

WHAT COULD BE a more Californian pastime than a walk in a mission garden?

The Mission San Gabriel Archangel and its lands once occupied almost the entire San Gabriel Valley. Founded in 1771, with its present building established in 1775, the mission developed over several decades.

Victoria Padilla's illustrated history, *Southern California Gardens*, describes for us the old mission gardens. According to her book, the padres in San Gabriel sent messengers to Mexico in 1784 for seeds and cuttings to plant at the new mission. From Sinaloa they brought oranges, lemons, figs, olives, pecans, grapes, pears and more.

By 1805, Padre Jose de Zalvidea was making the San Gabriel Mission a center of agriculture and richest of all the missions. The padres managed vineyards and citrus orchards, and in 1812 the wheat crop was 32,618 bushels—the largest from any mission. The rose hedges were practical and beautiful. Thornier still were the hedges

of prickly pear cactus (Opuntia tuna), up to twenty feet high, to keep grazing livestock out of the cultivated plots. The name of Las Tunas Drive recalls those hedges today, and remnants of them are still in the city.

Since water was scarce, flower gardens were limited. But with Padilla's historical notes you could create a "mission garden" corner in your own yard: hollyhocks, sweet peas, marigolds, madonna lilies, and more.

Today, the San Gabriel Mission gardens are like a labyrinth. You'll step in and out of little walled plots, finding a deep old water cistern, huge soap and tallow vats, a cluster of little open fireplaces. Perhaps a soft conversation in Spanish from fellow visitors will help to carry you back. Giant scalloped clam shells hold water here and there. The baked floor tiles of the quadrangle patio are two hundred years old.

This is not an authentically restored period garden. Instead, you'll find a casual mixture from across the centuries. The cactus garden contains varieties of opuntia, agaves, and cactus clusters looking like small furry animals. Mockingbirds, sparrows and mourning doves may set up a loud chorus.

Water for the original mission gardens was carried here by aqueducts from Wilson Lake to the north, long ago drained to become Lacy Park in San Marino. Clay pipes and open ditches called "zanjas" brought the water across the land.

Just beyond a low brick wall is the Campo Santo, a cemetery first consecrated in 1778. Here the dates and history of the mission gardens become more visible, as you linger to read the markers.

If you step into the high sanctuary of the old church, you'll find it cool within its thick walls. All is solid there now, since earthquake restoration was completed recently. Beautiful painted accents of green and dark red touch the columns and archways.

Two hundred years of history await your visit.

How to get there: The San Gabriel Mission is at 537 W. Mission Drive. From the 10 Freeway, exit at Del Mar Ave. and drive north. Turn left on Mission Drive. Call (626) 457-3035.

Church of Our Saviour

◇ San Gabriel ◇

THE LITTLE EPISCOPAL CHURCH was built in 1872, just a few orchards north of the San Gabriel Mission. Another mile to the north was the ranch of Benjamin D. Wilson, called Lake Vineyard. In this orbit of long ago lived three families, which were really one family: the Wilsons, the Shorbs, and the Pattons.

When you visit the Church of our Saviour today, you'll find evidence of these historic names. But how to keep them straight? You might remember this family group as Don Benito and the two sons-in-law (the first being J. DeBarth Shorb; the second, George Smith Patton, father of the World War II general.)

Wilson, known as Don Benito in California, was born in Nashville, Tennessee in 1811. Joining the Rocky Mountain Fur Company he traveled west, reaching the Los Angeles pueblo in 1841. Ten years later, he was elected the charter mayor of that city and bought a 200-acre property east of town which he called Lake Vineyard. Nothing remains of his house today, which was on the northern edge of San Marino's Lacy Park (then a small lake).

126

Later Wilson was a state senator of California, a successful vintner, a developer of Los Angeles harbor, and a visitor into the mountain range which now bears his name on Mount Wilson.

Meanwhile, the Rev. Henry Messenger, a former missionary to Liberia, had decided to build a new church in the San Gabriel Valley. Frances Dyer Vinton of Providence, Rhode Island, provided the funds and Wilson contributed two acres of his land for church and rectory. In 1872 the church was finished, of adobe bricks and hand-forged nails made at Lake Vineyard.

The bell (which still rings today) had come around Cape Horn from New England. Rev. Messenger was lodged for a time at the Wilsons' home.

Eventually the two sons-in-law were also associated with the church. James DeBarth Shorb, who married Wilson's daughter Sue, came to California from Emmitsburg, Maryland at age 21. He joined an oil exploration company, then called upon Wilson and met Sue. The two men shared years of business activity together. The Shorbs lived in a Victorian house where the present Huntington Art Gallery stands, less than a mile from Wilson's home.

Later George Smith Patton Sr. married Wilson's daughter Ruth. Their baby son George Jr., grandson of Don Benito, was baptized in the Church of our Saviour in 1886. Today, a life-sized bronze statue of him as Commander of the U.S. 15th Army stands just outside the church door.

In the 1950s a new section of the nave was added, north of the original church. Colorful windows glow, some made by the Judson Studios of the Arroyo Seco, two in the style of Tiffany, and several honoring the Pattons. In the very old cemetery outside, members of the church's founding families are at rest.

How to get there: The Church is at 535 W. Roses Rd, San Gabriel. From the 10 Freeway, exit at Del Mar Ave. and drive north; turn left on Roses Rd. Call (626) 282-5147.

Ramona Museum of California History

✧ *San Gabriel* ✧

IT TOOK THE Ramona Museum of California History a hundred years to get here, but they're here now—under the wings of the San Gabriel Mission and just a block from the San Gabriel Historical Museum.

This is the home of Ramona Parlor #109 (chartered 1887), the Native Sons of the Golden West. Members are native-born Californians, dedicated to preserving and marking historic places throughout our State. Early on, this Parlor (which is like a "Chapter") met at the Patriotic Hall on Figueroa Street in Los Angeles.

The members always loved collecting relics and artifacts from California history. Lacking their own museum, they stored their holdings in various places, such as the Banning Museum in Wilmington and the Los Angeles County Museum of Natural History, when it first opened in 1912.

So the collection was, you might say, in foster homes over the years. Meanwhile the Native Sons continued their work of placing historical markers and supporting historic causes.

In 1966 a bequest from member Edwin Fletcher made possible the construction of Fletcher Hall, in Highland Park just below the Southwest Museum. The building would be a meeting place and museum to reunite the scattered collections.

Some of the items never found their way back, but over 1000 pieces did return. Members tried to get a handle on what they had, but financial troubles intervened, and later the City of Los Angeles wanted their building for public use. The collections, accumulated during about a hundred years, would be on the move again.

Before the Native Sons had to leave Fletcher Hall, the energetic Rosemarie Lippman and Susan Gleason, now Director and Curator respectively, came to organize their museum pieces, which were to be stored.

More good luck was securing the present building on Mission Drive in San Gabriel, where the Native Sons opened their new Ramona Museum in November 1998.

The museum is small—two rooms and a few extra niches. Displays illustrate Native American, Mission, Rancho, and Statehood themes of California history. Since the space is compact, a "treasure hunt" approach to your visit might be fun. First, you can't miss John C. Fremont's carriage (1870). But can you find: an aerial photo of San Francisco in ruins just after the 1906 earthquake? the large Los Angeles town map drawn by E. Ord in 1849, with fields and vineyards pieced neatly beside the river? how about the crackling dipper (a five-foot long scoop, used for trying out whale oil at Portuguese Bend in 1869)?

Blacksmith's tools; someone's collection of tiny cream pitchers; an arrow-straightening stone among the Indian grinding stones? Then set your own treasure hunt, for your students or family members on the trail of discovery.

How to get there: The Museum is at 339 South Mission Dr. From the 10 Freeway, exit at Del Mar Ave. and drive north. Turn left on Broadway and left on Mission Dr. Call (626) 289-0034.

Heritage Park
✧ *Santa Fe Springs* ✧

EVERY COMMUNITY has ways of saving its history. Heritage Park in Santa Fe Springs has pulled together a cast of historical characters.

The Los Nietos Valley southeast of Los Angeles was granted to Corporal Jose Manuel Nieto in the 1780s. His lands reached from the Pacific Ocean to the Puente Hills, and from the Santa Ana River to the San Gabriel River.

Later Patricio Ontiveros arrived in the area. He had come with the first settlers to the pueblo of Los Angeles and was once overseer of the San Juan Capistrano cattle herds. About 1806 he built an adobe which appears later in our story.

In the 1870s Dr. H. E. Fulton purchased some of this same land, where today's Heritage Park now stands. Drilling a well, he hit sulphur waters and developed a thriving health resort with their curative powers. About 400 patients were treated annually, most of them

camping out in the pure air. Early travelers describe stopping at Fulton Wells for a drink of sulphur water.

Eli Hawkins acquired some of Fulton's land in 1877. There he created a fine estate with formal gardens and a glass conservatory for plants seldom seen in Southern California. His two-story Carpenter Gothic-styled barn was a local marvel at a cost of $5,000.

The Santa Fe Railroad line from Los Angeles to San Diego crossed Fulton's land in 1888. The peaceful river plains, formerly reached only by stage, were suddenly linked to a wider world. The Nimock family purchased the Hawkins home place, renamed it "Fairyland," and expanded its grounds to the Victorian taste of the 1890s.

Pastoral days, then agriculture, then the railroad—so far a familiar Southern California pattern. But in 1919 this community was turned upside down: oil! Settlers had been noticing strange happenings for years when drilling for water. Oil seepage had been a nuisance in pastures. But everything blew when Union Oil finally struck a gusher and the first well began producing 3000 barrels a day.

In the resulting boom, farmers fled while investors rushed in. Oil rigs sprouted in a mad mosaic of derricks and citrus trees. The modern city of Santa Fe Springs took off.

With the pace of change, everything was disappearing as quick as a gusher swallows an old farm wagon. To stem the tide, the town's citizens created Heritage Park in 1986. The basis was the old Hawkins-Nimock gardens.

There you'll see the ruins of the Ontiveros adobe, and a "dig" showing the family trash pit. From the Hawkins era is the reconstructed carriage barn, filled with exhibits and photographs. The conservatory and garden paths recall the Victorian age.

An old oil field office from the 1920s holds park staff, and just beyond the park are buildings of a new corporate center. So many periods of Santa Fe Springs history are here.

How to get there: From the 210 Freeway, drive south on the 605 Freeway, then east on Telegraph Road, right on Heritage Park Drive, and left on Mora Drive to 12100 Mora Drive. Call Heritage Park at (562) 946-6476.

Clarke Estate

◇ *Santa Fe Springs* ◇

LOVERS OF SOUTHERN CALIFORNIA ARCHITECTURE: do not miss the surprising Clarke Estate, designed by Irving Gill and now belonging to the city of Santa Fe Springs.

Gill's spare and distinctive style stands out like a voice recognized in a crowd. The 8,000 square-foot house he built for the Clarkes in 1921 is one of the best remaining examples of his work.

Irving Gill was a New Yorker who came to San Diego in 1893 at age 23. At the Hotel Del Coronado he met influential Easterners, including the landscape architect Frederic Law Olmstead, Jr. who com-

missioned Gill to design his house. Soon Gill's work was in demand.

In the 1910s and 20s, Gill's buildings showed Mediterranean or Mission Revival style, with arches and pergolas. But he also liked the International Style, with its abstract and simple forms. He wrote that architects should cast away ornamentation and concentrate instead on structural beauty.

He designed many small homes, experimenting with cubist

forms: some of these houses were literally little cubes. But for Chauncey and Marie Clarke, he expanded his design philosophy.

Chauncey Clarke, of Peoria, Illinois, had made two fortunes: from distilleries, then from Arizona gold mining. He and his wife came to California in 1904 and bought ranch properties. They commissioned Gill to build their home on 60 acres of citrus groves in Santa Fe Springs.

The house rambles in a well-ordered way. It is built entirely of poured-in-place reinforced concrete, around a central courtyard which is covered with canopies in the rainy season. Tuscan columns and arches surround the courtyard. Mayan designs are pressed into the concrete floor, and leaf shapes into the walls.

An Egyptian motif is painted around a fireplace, and Mayan-carved planters in the courtyard hold vines. Otherwise, the house has little decoration. Skylights and well-placed windows bring in the daylight.

The building's different levels and terraces remind us of Southwest pueblos. It seems to be simple and yet complex, at the same time—photogenic from every angle.

The Clarkes enjoyed their unusual house for just a few years. Then the increasing noise and smells from nearby oil wells became too unpleasant. They moved to the Coachella Valley and established a ranch called Point Happy Date Gardens. Chauncey Clarke died in 1926 and his wife in 1948.

A relative of the Clarkes lived in the house until 1986. That year the city of Santa Fe Springs bought the Clarke Estate as a historic landmark and now uses it for tours, meetings, and special events. The furnishings are new, but they have a 1920s feeling.

Several acres of gardens surround the house today. Sitting by the ornamental pool, you might think of other Southern California styles in the 1920's: the Spanish Colonial Revival, the Tudor bungalow, the woodsy late Craftsman. What an interesting surprise, this "voice" of Irving Gill in the conversation of architects.

How to get there: The Clarke Estate is at 10211 Pioneer Blvd. From the 605 Freeway, exit at Telegraph Rd. and drive east. Turn Right on Pioneer Blvd. Call (562) 868-3876.

Palmview Park Sabre Jet
✧ *West Covina* ✧

LOOKING A LITTLE like a beached whale, the Palmview Park Sabre Jet still retains its dignity as a proud veteran of the Korean War era. For nearly 40 years, it has been making memories for West Covina's children.

At rest now in a large sandbox, this F-86D Sabre Jet was donated by the U.S. Air Force to the City of West Covina in 1961. Every year the city's Park Maintenance Supervisor must send photographs to the Air Force, showing the good condition of the static display.

The Air Force also performs occasional safety inspections on the jet. Rumors that Snoopy has been seen piloting it have not disturbed its yearly approval by the U.S. military.

To become a well-loved playground feature, the jet had all instruments and gauges removed. It has been covered with a thin layer of gunnite, almost turning it from aircraft to sculpture. Its painted insignias and official number remain intact.

Short ladders have aided generations of youngsters to explore its tail fins or scamper along its back. The most fun is to climb into its seat, just a little pocket for one. Its mechanisms now have to be imaginary, for they are long gone. As a sandbox toy this seems like a giant, but as a plane it's surprisingly small, just a little runabout of the air. It must have maneuvered nimbly, in its day.

The family of Sabre Jets were the top performing jet fighters of their time. After test flights, the Air Force received the first one, the F-86A, in 1948. This promptly set a world speed record of 570 miles per hour.

The Sabres were the first swept-wing plane in the U.S. fighter inventory, and they could easily out-fly the straight-wing aircraft. Wing and tail were swept back 35 degrees.

As demand increased for the Sabres, North American Aviation opened two new production facilities: the former Curtiss-Wright plant in Columbus, Ohio, reminiscent of the Wright Brothers, and a new plant in Downey, California, which much later made the Apollo Spacecraft. Thus the Sabres were right in the middle of 20th century aviation history.

North American eventually manufactured over 6,000 Sabre Jets of all the models, developing this "family" of planes over two decades.

The West Covina jet is an F-86D, originally with a span of 37 feet, length of 41 feet, and height of 15 feet. Its top speed was 650 miles per hour, with a range of 1,000 statute miles. At work it carried 24 Mighty Mouse rockets in its fuselage. It is one of 2,540 of this model that were built.

All is quiet now for the West Covina jet. A six-year-old in a red shirt climbs up to go for a spin, and once again it takes to the skies.

How to get there: Palmview Park is at the corner of Lark Ellen Ave. and Puente Ave. From the 10 Freeway exit at Vincent Ave. and drive north; turn right on Puente Ave.

Bailey House
⟡ *Whittier* ⟡

REBECCA BAILEY WAS standing on the porch of her house beside the Puente Hills, looking west across the open Montebello plain toward Los Angeles. Faraway she could see the dust of an approaching horseman—her husband Jonathan and his horse Polly returning from a visit to town. The year was 1887.

You can stand on Rebecca's porch today, at the snug six-room ranch house that was Whittier's first residence. Still in its original location, it gives a keen sense of the presence of the Baileys, leaders of the original Quaker settlement there. The house had been built in the early 1870's as headquarters for the John Thomas ranch. Its dark green pepper trees at the base of the tawny hills could be seen for miles. Later, the Baileys could signal their relatives on Hill Street in Los Angeles by hanging a white sheet against those trees, visible by telescope.

In 1887, the Pickering Land and Water Company of Chicago purchased the 1,270-acre Thomas Ranch for a Quaker community in the West. The Baileys moved into the ranch house and the town's first religious services were conducted on the porch. Jonathan Bailey was 68, his wife 66.

You would have liked Rebecca Bailey. With water scarce and needed for the ranch, she arranged for the bathtub water to drain into her garden. Children loved to visit her and she kept a jar of sugar cookies near the kitchen door. On her bedroom wall is an embroidered motto, "Onward and Upward."

The house is simple, with basic comforts: heating by a small coal fireplace, water pump at the kitchen sink, the kerosene lamps. The interior is cool, dim and peaceful.

A photograph of Jonathan Bailey faces one of John Greenleaf Whittier across the sitting room. Jonathan, it is said, would hide a penny in his ample gray beard, then take a little child in his lap to search for it. In March 1892, the Baileys invited the whole settlement to their golden wedding anniversary. In the house a photo of this day shows all ages playing and dining under the pepper trees.

The house also serves as the collective memory of Whittier families, who often give a treasured item, saying "This should be in the Bailey House." These pieces are not "on display" but look like part of Rebecca's household: pearly salt dishes, or a silver hair brush.

The Bailey House, in dilapidated condition, was purchased by the City of Whittier in 1973 as a project honoring the nation's Bicentennial. Many volunteers accomplished the restoration. The city maintains the exterior and grounds as a park, where Rebecca Bailey's garden has been recreated based on period research. Plant lovers: take note.

The house, now on the National Register of Historic Places, is faithfully interpreted by volunteer docents, who will meet you—yes—on the porch.

How to get there: The house is at 13421 E. Camilla St. From the 605 Freeway, exit on Whittier Blvd. and drive east. Turn left on Hadley St., left on Painter Ave. and right on Camilla. Call (562) 945-3871.

Paradox Hybrid Walnut Tree
✧ *Whittier* ✧

FEW PEOPLE TODAY remember the walnut industry which once covered thousands of acres in the San Gabriel Valley. But a survivor and patriarch of those days still lives: the Paradox Hybrid Walnut Tree of Whittier.

This giant, now a California Registered Historical Landmark, was planted about 1907 by George Weinshank on the grounds of the Whittier State School. This trade school for boys was the first juvenile correction facility established in California (1890). Today it is called the Fred C. Nelles School.

Weinshank had learned trees from his father's business in Los Angeles. At the State School he taught agriculture to the boys and was in charge of the nursery. Later he operated his own nursery, specializing in walnuts.

WHITTIER'S OLD WALNUT TREE
1907

Early in this century, the School had leased two acres to the University of California for experiments in walnut culture. The site was along present Whittier Boulevard, then a narrow country road. The experts planted a dozen walnut varieties, with once-familiar names like Placentia Perfection, Eureka, Prolific, and the Paradox Hybrid (from Weinshank's own nursery).

In 1925, the University gave up the lease and soon after all the trees were pulled out but one. The Paradox Hybrid was such an exceptional grower that it was spared.

Seventy years ago, they thought the tree was large. Today, the patriarch spreads across more than 100 feet. To truly encounter this tree, you must go as close to the trunk as you can, then look up. Once the young walnut trees reached about ten feet, they were cut back to five feet, causing the wide branch system you see here.

English walnuts may have been planted by the Mission Fathers. The University of California *Journal of Agriculture* stated in 1915 that the industry then had a $45 million investment with about 50,000 acres and over a million trees statewide. At the height of walnut prosperity, Orange and Los Angeles counties led the state.

The nuts could be safely stored for twelve months or more, so business was far more stable than for perishable fruits. Production and prices were climbing. Said the U.C. Journal, "the walnut is being looked upon more and more as a necessary food by the people of this country."

As the groves aged, they gradually gave way to citrus in Whittier. Many old walnut trees fell over in the 1933 earthquake and could never be righted. By the 1940's housing and industry replaced the groves—all but the Paradox Hybrid.

The tree's last threat came in 1955, when State highway planners doomed it to widen Whittier Boulevard. It was saved by determined community groups, including the Native Daughters of the Golden West (with George Weinshank's four daughters among them).

Now the Whittier Art Association holds an art festival each spring beside the landmark tree.

How to get there: From the 605 Freeway, exit at Whittier Blvd. and drive east. The tree is opposite 12352 Whittier Blvd. Turn right just past tree to park on the frontage road. For information, call the Whittier Historical Museum: (562) 945-3871.

King Richard's Antique Center
⬧ *Whittier* ⬧

WHAT IS BIGGER than a breadbox and was full of oranges before people drank orange juice?

At 100,000 square feet, this building surely meets the first test. And built in 1903, it pre-dates the time when the golden fruit was first squeezed for juice. This is the Whittier Citrus Association Packing House, transformed in 1980 into King Richard's Antique Center. It now houses 300 spaces for individual antique dealers.

Any lover of Southern California history should visit this huge packing house, one of the few left. The current owners have strengthened it for modern use, but the signs of its age and its citrus past are plain to see. No wonder the project won the Whittier Conservancy annual award for outstanding restoration of a commercial structure.

The old packing process began when lumber was delivered at the bottom of the three-story building. The two-compartment wooden crates were made there (built strong to withstand train travel).

On the wall are posted some original labels for the three brands packed at this house: Greenleaf, Whittier, and Atta Boy.

A mechanical elevator operated by a horse carried the crates to the upper floors. On the main level 160 women sorted the fruit by size and quality. Each orange was individually wrapped in tissue paper stamped "Sunkist", the trademark name adopted in 1908 by the California Fruit Growers Exchange. That same year, as a promotional gift to customers, the company began offering its "Orange Blossom" pattern silverware in exchange for the tissues.

In the sorting hall, the ceiling joists leap such a wide span that architecture students come to study them today. The original skylights to conserve energy are still there, now with plastic panes.

The top floor had about 150 workers to arrange the fruit in the crates. Eventually, one area was for oranges and another for lemons. Two levels of unusual clerestory windows let light come pouring in. There was an early form of air conditioning: ventilating by a huge pipe through the ceiling, combined with fans. Outside the building ran two railroad lines to carry away the finished crates.

Offices in the old citrus house were tiny. The maximum space was needed for the packing. In the high season with the fruit ripening quickly, shifts worked through every bit of daylight, sometimes using foot-powered machines.

And the orange juice? This was virtually unknown until 1916, when Sunkist began its "Drink an Orange" campaign. The promotion included glass hand-juicers for 10 cents each. Soon the campaign had changed oranges from luxury items into a household staple across the country.

About 1940 fruit packing ended at the Whittier Citrus Association Packing House. After years as a warehouse or empty, it was finally restored. Looking past an unbelievable variety of antiques, you can plainly see the original building. It's huge; it's rare. Don't miss it.

How to get there: King Richard's Antique Center is at 12301 Whittier Blvd. From the 405 Freeway, exit at Whittier Blvd. and drive east to the corner of Penn St. For information, call (562) 698-5974.

Pio Pico State Historic Park
✧ *Whittier* ✧

TO IMAGINE THE early setting of the Pio Pico adobe, visualize a river, a wide valley, a mountain range beyond, and a thriving mission—all named San Gabriel.

All these affected the life of Pio de Jesus Pico, born at the San Gabriel Mission in 1801. Before his death in Los Angeles in 1894, he had lived through California's Mexican and American years, the secularizing of the missions, the land boom of the 1880's, and the birth of many new towns.

Pio Pico was of mixed Caucasian, African, Spanish and Indian heritage, one of ten children. He became a businessman and rancher. Serving in the government of Mexican California for nearly 20 years, he finally was the last Mexican governor of California when the Americans took over in 1846.

Pico was one of the few to keep his lands after the change to American rule. In the 1850s he and his brother Andres owned about 532,000 acres, including half the San Fernando Valley. In 1868, he sold 116,000 acres in San Fernando and with the proceeds built and furnished

Pico House, an elegant hotel still standing in El Pueblo de Los Angeles State Historic Park.

But Pico's favorite home was his Rancho Paso de Bartolo Viejo ("El Ranchito", his smallest property at 8,890 acres). Here on the east bank of the San Gabriel River, he began his adobe house about 1852. Over the next 20 years he added more rooms, built of straw-laced adobe bricks, covered with mud inside and out, then whitewashed with plaster of crushed limestone and seashells.

The roof was sealed with tar from La Brea, and the floors were of packed earth. Hides or wooden shutters covered the windows, which had no glass. Yet reports of visitors praised the carpets, paintings, and a carved rosewood piano.

The San Gabriel River was wild and free in those days. A flood in 1867 split the river and created a new branch, destroying some rooms of Pico's home. A great flood of 1884 undermined much of the rambling building. Most of what you see today was probably built after that deluge (the house rambled eastward this time, away from the river).

Pico died in poverty, having lost his adobe to debt. He was taken in by his daughter for his last years. Meanwhile the once pastoral San Gabriel Valley, watered by the fickle river, was being settled into towns. The declining Pico adobe was at last rescued and transferred to the State of California in 1917.

Today the concrete river channel intervenes harshly between Pio Pico's home and his birthplace at the San Gabriel Mission. But restoration is underway at the old house and a patch of green awaits your picnic at the State Historic Park.

How to get there: The park is immediately west of the 605 Freeway along Whittier Blvd. Exit the Freeway at Whittier Blvd. Signs direct to the Park entrance on Pioneer Blvd. Call (562) 695-1217.

Murphy Ranch Park

✧ *Whittier* ✧

MANY SUCCESS STORIES in early Southern California began with these questions: "Where is the water? And how can we get some?"

One person who answered these questions rather brilliantly was Simon J. Murphy, a lumberman from Detroit who came to Whittier in 1887. The region's land boom was still underway, as his group of Eastern speculators bought about 2000 acres of the Ramirez ranch in east Whittier. Fifty percent of the purchase price was still due.

Murphy had his subdivision maps drawn to sell the property quickly, but the bubble burst. Land values spiraled downward. He and his partner John Sanborn determined to stay with their property, but it was useless without water. Only a further gamble could save the investment.

Forming the East Whittier Land and Water Company, Murphy purchased 60 acres of water-bearing land in the San Gabriel River

bed at Bassett (near present-day Valley Boulevard). There, water came to the surface and Murphy built a system of redwood flumes from the river extending east on a timber trestle. The water flowed around the Puente Hills and south to the ranch.

The residents of Whittier shared this bounty, with allocations termed "one miner's inch of water per 10 acres of land." Some said the ingenious Murphy and his engineer A.L. Reed of Port Huron, Michigan, had managed to make water flow uphill.

The Murphy Ranch was profitably planted in citrus, and the family spent winters here in their Queen Anne-style Victorian home which still stands. Racehorses shipped from Michigan were also kept on the property.

The Murphy Oil Company was organized to develop oil found on the ranch, offsetting the last of Murphy's debts on the land and water ventures. In 1921 Simon J. Murphy Jr. established the Murphy Memorial Hospital in Whittier (now gone) to honor his father's contributions to the town.

In the 1940s the land was at last divided, as Murphy had hoped so long before. A section called Friendly Hills offered homes for country living, with complete orchard care available through the ranch management as these were peak years for the land's citrus production.

After World War II, more houses covered the old ranch. But today there is a remnant, the hilly and wild Murphy Ranch Park. These 48 acres became a city park in 1969, as a wooded canyon with equestrian and hiking trails. You can picnic at tables near the entrance, then wind your way upward. If you look closely you'll see a few citrus trees near the picnic area. Higher, a coyote may cross your path, keeping his distance.

How to get there: Murphy Ranch Park is at 16200 Las Cumbres Dr. From the 605 freeway, exit at Whittier Blvd. and drive east. Turn left on Colima Rd., then right on Youngwood Dr. to its end at Las Cumbres.

Clock, Claremont Train Station · Claremont California

Yorba-Slaughter Adobe
◇ *Chino* ◇

HISTORY SEEKERS, start early if it's a hot summer day. Then we can proceed undaunted to cross 150 years of time and step into the Yorba-Slaughter Adobe of Chino, built in 1852-53.

You'll be in the Prado Basin, a broad grassland watered with streams like Chino Creek and separated from the San Gabriel Valley by the Chino Hills. Here Jose Antonio Yorba was granted the 60,000-acre Rancho Santiago de Santa Ana in 1801. His son Bernardo added 18,000 acres known as Santa Ana del Chino, and his son Raimundo built the adobe home you can see today.

The house is beautifully sited on a small hill above Chino Creek. Just to the east, natural wetlands stretch along the creek, with seasonal flooding and habitat for migratory birds. The drive to reach the adobe still takes you through agricultural lands, with a welcome sense of open space.

The Yorba Adobe was a stage stop for the Butterfield Overland Mail between 1858 and 1863. Travel passed nearby on the much-used Fort Yuma to Los Angeles Road.

In 1868 Fenton Slaughter bought the adobe house and 3,000 acres around it. Born in Virginia, he was a veteran of the Mexican War of 1846. On these lands he raised cattle, Merino sheep, horses, grain, and grapes. A small settlement known as Rincon grew up there, most of it now gone, with post office, general store, dairy, and winery. Fenton Slaughter served in the state legislature and as a supervisor of San Bernardino County.

After Slaughter's death in 1897, the adobe gradually declined. Finally, only one of his ten children took an interest in saving it: Julia Slaughter Fuqua. Through her efforts, the house was restored beginning in 1929 and donated to San Bernardino County in 1971 with about two acres of land.

It's unusual, this house, among California's nineteenth century adobes. It had many exterior doors and windows, and wide porches on all four sides. There were no fireplaces. Originally there were four rooms on the main floor and three above in a sleeping loft. In the house, photographs show that a violent windstorm of the 1930's destroyed the upper story, leaving the building already half "torn down".

At this point, only Julia Fuqua could persuade the family that it was worth saving. Today, you'll find inside Fenton Slaughter's law books (he was self-taught), many pieces of the family's furniture, and Julia's formal black dress showing a tiny waist. Note the ingenious way the Slaughters expanded their dining table as the family grew. A loveseat carved from a grapevine is just one of the curious heirlooms.

An extension of the house, built about 1909, was used as the main residence for a time, while the aging adobe was used to grow mushrooms (a testament to the sheltering coolness of those adobe walls).

How to get there: The Adobe is at 17127 Pomona Rincon Road. From the 60 Freeway, exit at Euclid Ave. and drive south, turn right on Pine Ave. and left on Pomona Rincon Road. For information, call (909) 597-8332.

Rancho Santa Ana Botanic Garden
✧ *Claremont* ✧

AT AGE 70, a garden is just in its prime—although this one has already moved once in its life.

Rancho Santa Ana Botanic Garden (known as RSABG) is an 86-acre preserve of California native plants near the Claremont Colleges. A prettier spot you could not find to see the passing blooms and shades of each season.

The garden originated with a pioneer Southern California family. John W. Bixby of Maine and his wife Susan Hathaway Bixby developed the vast Rancho Los Alamitos, now the city of Long Beach. Their daughter, Susanna, was born on the ranch in 1880. Later she lived a Bohemian life on San Francisco's Russian Hill, and married Dr. Ernest Bryant after a whirlwind romance.

In 1925, through an inheritance, she became sole owner of the 6,000 acre Rancho Santa Ana in Orange County. Soon she converted some of the hilly pastureland into a preserve for the California native plants she loved.

Mrs. Bryant's dreams linked her to the major botanists of her day. Theodore Payne advised her about her "Wild Garden project." Ralph Cornell, a famed landscape architect, urged her to establish a park for native plants. Willis Jepson, whose *Manual* of California plants is still a "Bible" today, wrote to her often. Even Frederick Law Olmstead, designer of New York's Central Park, laid out a scenic road on her ranch.

In 1927 she opened to visitors her garden of native plants in Santa Ana Canyon, Orange County. The *Christian Science Monitor* featured it in a 1933 article.

After Mrs. Bryant's death in 1946, family and advisors decided to affiliate the garden with the Claremont Colleges. An 86-acre site, on part of the historic Indian Hill mesa, proved ideal. In 1951, they started anew by setting out over 10,000 plants and about 25,000 bulbs there.

A home demonstration garden was completed in 1961. By 1965 the RSABG had all the oaks native to California plus about 1,350 other species. The place became lively with birds, and visitors today can request a bird check list in the Garden Shop.

The present garden has three areas: the Indian Hill Mesa, the East Alluvial Gardens (including plants of desert and dunes), and the 55-acre Plant Communities section deep at the back. Along the east and north are fine oak groves.

On the mesa, spring's flowers seem to favor yellows (poppies, monkeyflowers, yarrow, and flannel bush) and blues (iris, ceanothus, blue-eyed grass, a gorgeous purple mallow, and blue-flowered salvia as tall as you are). Pink clouds of coral bells are under the oaks. Look also for the pale ivory poppies like full moons. If you visit in other seasons, you'll find each has its own rewards.

How to get there: The RSABG is at 1500 N. College Ave. From the 10 Freeway, exit at Indian Hill Blvd. and drive north, turn right on Foothill Blvd. and left on College Ave.
Call (909) 625-8767.

Claremont Railroad Depot
◇ *Claremont* ◇

DO YOU KNOW where your local train depot is tonight?

Some gems of Southern California depots are gone now, leaving just the ghosts of photographs behind. Others may be turned into a museum, a restaurant, or put up on blocks in transit to becoming something else.

Claremont's depot, built by the Atchison, Topeka, and Santa Fe Railroad in 1927, has had a luckier fate. Brought back from emptiness and now active again with Metrolink and bus services, it can smile at the joke of being re-named a "multi-modal transportation hub."

It was the Pan American-California Exposition at Balboa Park (San Diego) in 1915 that started a vogue for Spanish Colonial Revival architecture. The columns and arches, towers, tile roofs, and decorated portals against plain walls became the rage in Southern California. Through the 1920s, many of the region's Victorian railroad stations were replaced by depots in the new style.

Claremont had been virtually created by the Santa Fe Railroad, which promoted the new town to sell land along the railway line. In 1887, the company connected Chicago and Los Angeles by a route along the old Santa Fe Trail—through Kansas, Albuquerque, northern Arizona, Cajon Pass and San Bernardino. A Gothic-style train station was built in Claremont that year which stood until 1928.

In the 1890s young Pomona College settled in Claremont and also the town's first citrus association was established. Soon the Claremont depot became busy with oranges, lemons, and students. Packing houses lined the Santa Fe tracks nearby. The present depot saw the peak citrus production years, the 1920s through the 1950s.

And in the 1920s there were two new colleges in town: Claremont Graduate School (1925) and Scripps College (1926). The new depot was echoed by new civic buildings also in the Spanish Colonial Revival style: the original library (now gone), the post office, Chamber of Commerce and firehouse.

In 1967, the Santa Fe ended its passenger service through Claremont. The depot was closed and boarded up. At last, the city of Claremont purchased the building in 1989 to live again as a transit center for the area.

Today you'll see this choice little building restored with historic care. Its two-story tower has highly decorated doorways on north and south sides. The main waiting room and the western wing have Moorish shaped openings; the eastern wing once housed baggage operations. Vandalism, including a fire in 1968, caused interior damage, but decorative tiles have been recreated and wooden doors with the Santa Fe cross have been replaced.

The stenciled, beamed ceiling is original, as are the wooden balconies under the arched windows and the wrought iron ticket window. Landscapers have scattered flowering plants with a generous hand around the depot. Vibrant bougainvilleas in bloom add a fitting zest to this Spanish Colonial survivor.

How to get there: From the 10 Freeway, exit at Indian Hill Blvd. and drive north. Turn right on First Street and drive two blocks. For information, call Claremont Heritage at (909) 621-0848.

Grove House at Pitzer College
✧ *Claremont* ✧

THIS MAY BE one of the best house-moving stories you have heard.

It begins peacefully enough, with the scent of orange blossoms around a big brown shingle house in Claremont. Built in 1902 for the Stephens family, the house stood near the Red Line, with trollies running as far as Santa Monica Beach twice a day. Later the Zetterberg family bought the house and the surrounding groves.

As the town grew, the retirement community of Pilgrim Place eventually owned the Zetterberg House, using it for a meeting spot.

Meanwhile, at Pitzer College, newest of the Claremont colleges, Professor Barry Sanders was giving his course on the Arts and Crafts Movement. It was 1974, and the college still had no student gathering place on campus. On its eastern side, the college held a rough patch of land, not yet developed.

Someone in the course had an idea, the kind that is powerful enough and right enough to outlast any problems: let's find an Arts and Crafts-style house and move it to campus to be a student center.

The Zetterberg House (later called the Grove House) was offered to Pitzer College for $1. The president, board, and faculty of the college all approved. It would take five years to get all the permits and the funding for the move.

In 1977 the new foundation was built, but the house could not be moved on a State highway, which ruled out Foothill Blvd. What about the railroad right-of-way?

The Santa Fe had an eight-hour space in its train schedule and said yes, within that "window." So the house, cut in three pieces, traveled to Pitzer College along the tracks.

But there the foundation was deemed too close to the campus clock tower. For a year and a half the house sat off its foundation, covered with tarps. Patience ran thin. Finally the board of the college, and the city, both said, "This derelict has to go!"

At the last hour, the family of a student made a generous contribution that saved the project. They also helped to furnish the house in Craftsman style.

Today the Grove House, 3500 square feet, seems like "home" to anyone who steps in. Good smells come from the kitchen which serves lunch and dinner daily to college and towns people. Students read on the veranda or work in the citrus grove and native gardens beside the house.

Upstairs is a poetry room, a women's studies center, and a guest room for visiting parents. One student has made the house some stained glass windows, another a Craftsman-style lamp.

Pitzer College still offers studies of the historic Arts and Crafts period. And students find in the Grove House not only an artistic example, but one of the most valuable life lessons: "this can be done!"

How to get there: The Grove House is within the Pitzer College campus, south of Foothill Blvd. For information and directions, call (909) 621-8219.

Russian Village
✧ *Claremont* ✧

THERE IS SO MUCH to learn from history. Consider this story of the Depression, an earthquake, a flood, and the creation of a neighborhood.

At the age of 18, young Konstany Stys left his native Poland and came to the United States, becoming a steel worker in Youngstown, Ohio. In the early 1920's he came west with his wife to Claremont, where laborers were needed for building the Claremont Colleges.

As his family grew, he bought property along Mills Avenue in 1923, which was quite separate then from the town center and the colleges. Here he began to build houses eventually called the "Russian Village." In the Depression, Stys sold off parcels of his land cheap: "when you can pay," he said, or $10 per month. He welcomed the hardy and the ingenious, for they were building with salvaged materials.

The village was actually misnamed, perhaps because citizens mistook Stys's accent. But the name stuck, and work progressed.

After the Long Beach earthquake of 1933, Stys took trucks to the quake-damaged buildings, brought back assorted rubble, and dumped it at the end of the street for his neighbors to take. From condemned school buildings in Placentia, he brought roof tiles.

Field stones came from the clearing of nearby citrus groves. These were put in two huge piles at each end of the property for all to use. The red sandstone in one village house came from the demolished old court house in Los Angeles.

All this was a communal venture for Stys and his neighbors. He built a house for his family, then helped others with theirs. There was little money, but there were recycled telephone poles for columns and beams, and the "form lumber" cast aside from concrete work at the colleges.

The disastrous flood of 1938 provided a fine source: sidewalk rubble and torn-up street pavement to use for walls. Scrap sheet metal could become gates, and native stones were used as curbs.

Few if any of the houses had architectural plans, and Stys himself was untutored in this art, having probably only a grade-school education. Nevertheless, a spontaneous and creative style unites the little neighborhood. Sharing his salvaged "wealth," Stys left his touch on each of the dwellings.

For a while there was an informal association of the residents. These were tradesmen or artisans, people who could build a house. Today the owners are teachers, artists, and others, including one of the original families. The Russian Village is listed on the National Register of Historic Places.

The fourteen houses are called folk architecture now: made by hand and determination, in a time when nothing was wasted.

How to get there: These are private homes and can be seen only by a walk in the neighborhood. The houses are in the 300 block of Mills Avenue. From the 10 Freeway, exit at Indian Hill Blvd and drive north. Turn right at Arrow Hwy and right again on Mills. Park on a side street. Claremont Heritage has information at (909) 621-0848.

Olmec Head

✧ *Covina* ✧

IT IS STRANGELY DISORIENTING to look into a face that is taller than an average man.

Serene and mysterious, the great stone head is firmly planted in front of the Covina Police Station. A plaque identifies it as "Colossal Olmec Head #5. Tenochtitlan, Veracruz to the City of Covina. From the people and government of Veracruz on the 25th Anniversary of our Sister Cityhood, 1989" Nearly seven feet tall and weighing seven and a half tons, the gift was sent to Covina by its sister city Xalapa in Mexico.

In the 1940's the Smithsonian Institution and the National Geographic Society were jointly exploring the ancient Olmec civilization on the southern shore of the Gulf of Mexico. They discovered sixteen colossal stone heads, carved between 1200 and 900 B.C., and numbered them in the order of discovery. Covina's is a replica of number 5.

The Olmec culture was earlier than the civilizations of the Maya and Toltecs, and probably influenced them. One anthropologist calls the Olmec "the people of the jaguar" as they frequently depict that animal to symbolize cosmic and political power.

The Olmec were engineers as well as artists, for the gigantic heads were found 60 miles from the nearest source of their basaltic stone, across swampland and twisting trails. How the stone was moved remains a mystery.

The heads each have distinctly different faces and may represent individual rulers. If so, they are the earliest political portraits known in the Americas.

The replica of Head #5 was also carved in basalt and is an exact copy of the original. With modern tools, it was made in nine months. The head wears a helmet with a stylized representation of an eagle, the three claws toward the front. The slanted eyes were considered a sign of beauty in Pre-Columbian cultures. The full lips, the broad nose and brow, express dignity in the language of stone.

The Governor of Veracruz donated the replica to Covina in 1989. Before it could travel, Mexican archaeologists were summoned to make sure the head was not the original (which is now in the Museum of Anthropology of Xalapa).

For months the head rested in Covina storage. Then in July 1990 it was installed and dedicated in a festive ceremony. Today it is one of only two such replicas found outside the Mexican Republic.

In Mexico's tropical south, Olmec workers had dragged huge boulders through wetlands, probably by sledges, then sculpted them into the mysterious heads some three thousand years ago. Here, in Covina, the replica rests in modern landscaping.

In this tale of two cities—Xalapa and Covina—the Olmec head is a presiding spirit, keeping the secret of its strange melancholy.

How to get there: The Covina Police Dept. is at 444 Citrus Ave. From the 210 Freeway, drive south on the 605 Freeway. Exit on Ramona Blvd. and drive east, continuing as Ramona becomes San Bernardino Road. Just past Citrus Ave. turn right into the Police Dept. parking lot. For information: (626) 858-4408.

Firehouse Museum & Heritage House
◇ *Covina* ◇

THE COVINA VALLEY Historical Society has two historic sites open to visitors. You can see both in one exploratory afternoon—if you call ahead to determine the days both are open.

Your first stop would be the Firehouse-Jail Museum, located directly north of City Hall. This little Mission style building, built in 1911, looks like a miniature fire station. It's a bit hidden behind modern civic buildings. Step inside and you'll find small jail cells, stacked with the Historical Society's archives.

The rest of the building holds the collective memory of a town that grew up on citrus. Themes include the lore of the orange, the two World Wars, and pictures of Ellen Beach Yaw, the local singer known as Lark Ellen.

In a few minutes' drive, you can reach the 1908 residence called Heritage House. For three generations this Craftsman-style dwell-

ing belonged to the Nash family, owners of a Covina pharmacy. In 1989 the house was moved to its present spot within a park.

The 13-room house was built the same year as Pasadena's Gamble House. Like many early homes, it has some design features so convenient we have to ask: "Why don't our houses have that any more?"

For example: window seats with storage cupboards underneath, the ironing board within the kitchen wall, pocket doors between rooms (they disappear into the walls and don't stand in the way). Neatest of all is a double bed that slides through the wall into adjacent attic space, leaving just enough sticking out to be a "sofa" by day.

All this and a plate rail in the dining room. And a screened sleeping porch, once so popular in our hospitable climate. Those Covina orange groves were laden with fragrance on a summer night.

You'll see the skilled handwork of an earlier day, before television claimed so much of our time. The black beaded "walking dress" has fine detail. Several examples of "crazy quilting" (intricate mosaics of odd-shaped pieces) are embroidered with fancy stars. You can imagine a thousand evenings of work on these, with family members sitting and talking together.

Note too a paper collage cut from many steel engravings, called "The Four Seasons", in the parlor. Hand-snipped tiny parts have created a fantasy landscape.

For something to read while the ladies are stitching, the gentlemen might have stepped into the snug library, a miniature room ten feet square. The glass-fronted bookcases now contain books all dated before 1915. Doubtless the ladies also enjoyed this little treasure-box of a room.

How to get there: The Firehouse-Jail Museum is at 125 E. College Street (from the 210 Freeway, exit at Citrus Ave., drive south, turn left on College). Heritage House is at 300 N. Valencia Street (return on College to Citrus, turn left, then right on Badillo St. and right on Valencia). Contact the Covina Valley Historical Society at (626) 966-3978.

Covina City Park

✧ *Covina* ✧

IT WAS TREES, that March day in 1927, that brought together the citizens of Covina.

The project was beautification of the City Park, ten acres bought by the City in 1921 from the Adams ranch. For some years, the park was dusty and rough, just remains of the old orange grove that had once flourished there.

The Covina Lions Club was a major force in the park's history. They started a Fourth of July picnic tradition there in 1923, with a horse race down unpaved Badillo Street. Later, the Lions built a concrete bandstand for summer concerts.

In 1927, according to the local newspaper, the *Argus*, "half a hundred men and women, representing the civic clubs of the city, put over in a big way the planting of trees and shrubs" in the city park. Each group planted two or three trees. The men donned overalls and

the ladies their aprons. The shifts of workers changed during the day, as citizens could spare an hour or two from their usual tasks.

Charles G. Adams, a Los Angeles landscape architect, gave his services to help choose the 383 trees and shrubs. He had also supervised the grounds of the Kellogg ranch in nearby Pomona, now part of Cal Poly Pomona.

The groups planting that day were the Woman's Club, the Business and Professional Women, the Rotary, Lions, American Legion and Men's Club, and the Chamber of Commerce. All returned the next day to complete the project.

A photographer caught the sense of fun in the hard-working crew. And who was prouder than the fellow whose planting hole swallowed him as far as his vest pockets? In the background of the picture appears the popular bandstand.

Over the years the park was a summer haven. The seasonal opening of the plunge was celebrated each year in May, with music and picnics. The Municipal Band was first launched in the 1880s, then reborn in 1956 as the present Covina Concert Band. Its 40 musicians, under Dr. William Nicholls, now play free summer concerts in the park.

Summers at Covina Park also include a Tuesday evening film festival, family fun nights on Wednesdays, Senior Bingo, and a different musical group every Monday. The Lions Club is still at the fore, and where once were orange groves, children can play on a historic fire engine or a Cinderella pumpkin coach at the playground.

The park holds many memories, some of them told by local historian Pauline Ott, who recalls as one of the loveliest days of her life stepping off the Santa Fe train from Tennessee in 1919, at age 10, and seeing the San Gabriel valley for the first time: "a fairyland." She was there for that Fourth of July horse race, and enjoys Covina Park to this day.

How to get there: Covina Park is at Fourth St. and Badillo. From the 210 Freeway, exit at Citrus Ave. and drive south. Turn right on Badillo. Call Covina Park and Recreation Dept. at (626) 858-7271.

Holy Trinity Church
✧ *Covina* ✧

THE HISTORY OF THIS picturesque Covina church includes a wild windstorm, an earthquake...and more recently, a near Noah's Ark experience.

Covina itself was born from land speculation in Southern California's "Boom of the Eighties." In the 1880's, settlements sprang up along the San Gabriel River, tapping its waters for their agriculture. The Covina Irrigating Company of 1886 provided for citrus culture and the thriving new town.

In 1889 Covina's Holy Trinity Episcopal Church was formally established. A church building was erected in 1891, but within weeks it was blown down by fierce winds.

Using a larger wooden church in the interim, the congregation

prospered and finally sought a more permanent ark. Sketches of English village churches were brought back to Covina by the rector of the parish, and in 1910 their stone and shingle Eastlake-style church was complete, designed by Arthur B. Benton.

Benton was the architect of

Riverside's Mission Inn, and also the Mission Playhouse (now the Civic Auditorium) in San Gabriel. For the Anglicans, he departed from his usual Mission revival style, to create this corner landmark. In present day Covina, it stands out as crisply as a British voice in a Southern California conversation.

In 1950, the congregation added a new Parish Hall and offices. The patio and memorial gardens were created in 1967. Today, thirty years later, mature trees there offer refreshing shade.

Benton's church is of rich brown shingles and dressed stones from the San Gabriel River. Scottish masons transformed the river cobbles from their natural roundness. The masons built a solid foursquare tower with corner buttresses, and made neatly-fitted walls.

Inside, the woodwork and stained glass windows may make you feel you've just stepped in from your English walking tour.

But natural forces struck again in the 1990 earthquake, with the bell tower suffering major damage. The tower was rebuilt at a cost of over $100,000, and the mortgage for this effort was joyfully burned at the parish picnic of June 1997.

And what made the animals gather recently at Holy Trinity Church? It's somewhat of a mystery. But raccoons and opossums got into the insulation that lined the church's air conditioning ducts. The critters were so persistent that many had to be caught and safely released where they could not chew on buildings.

The present rector recalls a raccoon so large it put its paws up on her office windowsill. With outdoor vents now sealed and interior floorboards pried up, then replaced, the "canticle of the creatures" is over but not forgotten.

Holy Trinity Church welcomes visitors. A call ahead will ensure the snug sanctuary with an English accent will be open for you to see.

How to get there: The church is at 100 N. Third Ave., corner of Badillo Ave. From the 210 Freeway, exit at Citrus Ave. and drive south. Turn right on Badillo to Third. Call (626) 967-3939.

La Verne Heritage Park

◇ *La Verne* ◇

A HUNDRED YEARS AGO, putting together a windmill was just a part of life in Lordsburg, California. Today, Lordsburg is named La Verne, and the windmill is a minor triumph, recently dedicated as part of La Verne Heritage Park.

Lordsburg was a project of Isaac W. Lord, a speculator who built a 130-room hotel east of San Dimas in the land boom of the 1880's. "In those days a good hotel was half of a town," observed historian Harris Newmark. Completed in 1889, the hotel foundered when the boom went out and it never had a paying guest. Eventually it was sold to the German Baptist Brethren for a college. The imposing Victorian building, which resembled San Diego's Hotel del Coronado, is gone now—but the school is today's University of La Verne.

Contemporary with the hotel was a simpler dwelling, near the foothills. T. S. Oldham homesteaded there and built a small frame house of solid oak beam construction. Its outlines recall a Maine farmhouse, modest and strong. Tall windows have arched tops, and the front porch invites any visitor to "sit a spell."

This was citrus land, eventually a 120 acre ranch. John Weber purchased the house and property in 1900. His family and later the ranch foremen lived there for 80 years. In 1979, as the town (now La Verne) grew, the house stood empty, then was bought by developers.

But volunteer efforts saved "the house as old as Lordsburg". The La Verne Heritage Foundation was formed and the plucky little building was moved just half a mile, to a new city park.

Like many early Southern California buildings, this one had been moved before. In 1920 Weber, his son, and several mules pushed and pulled it about 50 yards from its original spot. In 1984, the house settled down in the present La Verne Heritage Park. A barn of its same vintage was moved nearby in 1989. And then came the windmill.

This eye-catching sentinel is a Dempster windmill, manufactured in Beatrice, Nebraska. The company, still in business there, has been operating for a century. The windmill lay in sections at Heritage Park for eight years, then was reconstructed like a giant jigsaw puzzle and dedicated under a harvest moon.

The blue-gray house and white barn stand amid citrus and old California pepper trees. The house is sometimes closed for restoration, but its surrounding park is a fine picnic spot.

The La Verne Heritage Foundation sponsors several annual events: a Pumpkin Patch in early October, orange picking in January, and summer concerts. The most fun of all might be joining the work to bring the house and a barnful of farm equipment back to life.

How to get there: La Verne Heritage Park is at 5001 Via De Mansion. Take the Foothill Freeway east to its end, continuing on Foothill Blvd. Turn north on Wheeler Ave., then east on Via De Mansion. For information, call (909) 593-2862.#

Graber Olive House

⟡ *Ontario* ⟡

HOW MANY STATES in the United States produce olives? Just one: California.

These tasty oval fruits are an ancient food, native to Asia Minor and cultivated since the beginning of historical times. In Greek mythology, Athena gave the olive to mankind, and the Bible records that, after the Great Flood, a dove brought an olive branch back to Noah.

Like most plants so useful and with such a long history, the olive has migrated near and far. In 1769 the Spanish padres brought it to the San Diego mission. From these trees were developed some of the best kinds for eating and for oil (several hundred varieties of olives are known today).

Maybe so, but Clay City, Indiana, where Clifford C. Graber was born in 1873, had no knowledge of olives. The young man worked in

his father's brickyard there, and then moved to Ontario, California with his brother Charles in 1892 to benefit their health.

They had arrived in a "model colony" plotted out by George Chaffey, an engineer from Ontario, Canada. The town had a beautiful divided boulevard, still tree-shaded today, running north from the Southern Pacific Railroad line. On a 10-acre lot, the brothers first lived in a tent in their orange groves. They supplemented their income selling vegetables and pickling a few olives in wooden kegs.

Later, Clifford built a big redwood house for his bride Georgia Bell and their four children. It is still occupied by members of the family, and the business continues where it has been since the 1890s.

By 1929, olives had won out over oranges, and the 1903 family barn was devoted to cannery operations. In the earlier days, customers could drive (in carriages or cars) up to a slot on the side of the barn, deposit their money, and pick up their canned olives from a stack nearby.

Over the years, Clifford Graber developed many ingenious methods in his olive preparation, including a grader which sorted the fruit by size and was powered by a Model T Ford motor. The tree-ripened olives still go through a process originally drawn from the farm journals with advice from UC Davis. The Grabers use the Manzanillo variety, descended from the Mission trees.

Visitors to Graber Olive House can tour the barn and see how the canning is done. The olives come in the fall, through December, from the 80-acre Graber ranch north of Porterville used since houses replaced the Ontario groves. The fruit is sorted, then cured in brine in 550 cement vats. Big boilers fire up to sterilize the cans. Up to 50,000 cans of olives are put up during a peak weekend. All this is carried on in the weathered old wooden barn, in its original spot.

A small museum on the property shows, in historic photographs and old farm objects, just how C. C. Graber looked beyond Southern California's citrus groves and saw the future of olives.

How to get there: Graber Olive House is at 315 E. 4th St., Ontario. From the 10 Freeway, exit at Euclid Ave. and drive south. Turn left on 4th St. For information, call (909) 983-1761.

Ontario Museum of History & Art
◇ *Ontario* ◇

THE HISTORY OF ONTARIO is stored in a building with its own layers of history. It's a fitting spot to show you both the expected (the citrus past of this "model colony") and the amusingly unexpected.

Two Canadian brothers, George and William Chaffey, founded the city of Ontario in 1882 with a dream. Their new town would be based on a mutual water company, and each colonist would receive one share of the water company with every ten acres of land.

It was to be an agricultural model for other settlements, recognized as such by the U.S. Congress in 1902. A scale model of the town's irrigation system appeared at the 1904 World's Fair in St. Louis.

Oranges and lemons were Ontario's pride in the early years. From the 1880s to the 1920s, the community worked cooperatively in growing and packing. The museum has a good showing of citrus artifacts,

from the smudge pots (vital to chase off the frosts) to picking tools and crate labels. This is familiar Southern California lore: it's a layer of history shared by many neighboring towns.

And the surprise exhibit? In 1904 Ontario housewives (and perhaps their husbands) were trying out electric irons, unhappy with the new-fangled things because they didn't heat all the way to the point. "I prefer my sad irons," said one, referring to the heavy non-mechanized irons left on the stove top to heat.

Earl Richardson of Ontario invented the first electric iron that would heat to its point, and named this creation Hotpoint. Soon his Pacific Electric Heating Company merged with General Electric, and Ontario produced generations of Hotpoint irons until 1982, in a building now just south of the museum.

If you never thought irons were fascinating, take a look at the sequence of about 40 of these homely items on display, spanning from 1904 to 1972. It's the life we led. The iron you first learned to iron with is in there somewhere.

And the building? This was once the City Hall, completed in 1936 by the Works Projects Administration (WPA), a government agency created by President Franklin D. Roosevelt to provide employment in the Depression years. WPA buildings are another layer of our history, with some 116,000 of them completed nationwide. Most were public buildings, including many post offices which survive today. At its peak, the WPA had close to 3.5 million people on its payroll.

Ontario's City Hall, now Museum, shows the grace of 1930s architecture. Built in lean times, it relies on simplicity. Yet its classical lines (here with a Spanish accent) and decorated doorways are very pleasing.

New exhibits will be added as the Museum grows into its commodious space. From smudge pots to irons, olives to roses, the history of Ontario is here to uncover, layer by layer for a hundred years.

How to get there: The museum is at 225 S. Euclid Ave. From the 10 Freeway, exit at Euclid and drive south. Call (909) 983-3198.

La Casa Primera Adobe
✧ *Pomona* ✧

IF YOU KEEP HISTORY FILES, chances are you have one for adobes—those practical earthen homes, cool in our hot summers, which once dotted the San Gabriel Valley. The adobes were likely to return to the earth, after years of weather, earthquakes and changing fortunes. Those that have survived are well worth a visit.

Historically, each adobe belonged to one of the early ranchos. The city of Pomona grew up on the Rancho San Jose and eventually surrounded the earliest home in the area, now called La Casa Primera (the "First House"), built soon after 1837.

For more than sixty years, the San Gabriel Mission had administered its vast surrounding lands. But after secularization of the missions in 1834, the Mexican Governor of California, Juan Alvarado, could grant these rich lands to private citizens.

Two young men from the Pueblo of Los Angeles appealed for a grant of 22,000 acres, which they received in 1837. They had been

working partners, running their cattle on much smaller holdings. The Rancho San Jose was granted to Ygnacio Palomares (age 26 that year) and Ricardo Vejar. Palomares received the upper portion, called San Jose de Arriba, and Vejar claimed the lower, San Jose de Abajo.

Palomares built a simple one-story adobe (La Casa Primera), with a covered walkway along one side. Here he and his family lived for 17 years, until they moved to the larger Palomares Adobe, still standing on Arrow Highway. Don Ygnacio's son, Don Francisco Palomares, then occupied the first little house.

Rancho San Jose prospered as the Gold Rush brought a growing population into California. Beef from the ranch was in demand, and the Mexican cattle also provided hides, horns, and tallow. But troubles swept through Southern California in the 1860s: severe flooding in 1861, which collapsed many adobe buildings, followed by two years of drought, winds, and grasshoppers.

The Vejar family finally lost their holdings in foreclosure, but the northern portion of the rancho had better luck. The magic touch of the Santa Fe Railroad, built through in 1886, increased land values there by up to 500 percent. In the real estate boom of the 1880's, a Palomares Hotel was built and even a new town of Palomares was announced, which never materialized. But the village of Pomona began to grow, as the Pomona Land and Water Company sold nearly 5,000 lots for new residents.

Through all of these changes, the little "First House" somehow survived. The president of the Land and Water Company owned it for years. Today, the Historical Society of the Pomona Valley cares for La Casa Primera.

When you visit, think about the handsome spread of hills and creeks which once surrounded it, the rancho of the young partners Palomares and Vejar.

How to get there: La Casa Primera is at 1569 North Park Ave. From the 10 Freeway, exit at Garey Avenue, drive north to McKinley Ave., turn left, then left on Park Ave. Call the Historical Society of the Pomona Valley at (909) 623-2198.

John Rains House
◇ *Rancho Cucamonga* ◇

IT'S A SURPRISE, this snug brick house, with ample windows providing light and air. Built in 1860, it is the same vintage as the scattered adobes on Southern California ranchos. Yet it too was built of the local native earth.

The Rains House, also known as the Casa de Rancho Cucamonga, was built for John Rains. He was originally from Alabama, served in the Texas Rangers in the Mexican-American War, then arrived in California in 1849. In 1856 he married Maria Merced Williams, already wealthy at age seventeen, and soon after he purchased the Rancho Cucamonga.

The rancho was originally a 13,000 acre grant from Governor Juan Alvarado to Tiburcio Tapia, who prospered there with his cattle and a winery. His adobe house, now gone, was on nearby Red Hill, source of the excellent clay used in the Rains House. The land was liberally watered by springs along the nearby foothills.

Brick masons from Ohio made the burned bricks (kiln-dried) for the house. Limestone deposits had been discovered just to the east,

174

for making the mortar. Even the interior walls were all solid brick. The original flat roof was covered by tar from the pits in Los Angeles.

But just two years later, in 1862, John Rains—who had aspired to politics but lost money with his cattle—was dead: murdered in a deed yet unsolved. Merced continued on at the Rancho, marrying Ramon Carrillo and eventually raising nine children.

The dramas of this strong-willed family make an absorbing tale, told by Rains House guides as portraits of the characters look down from the walls.

Over the years, the house passed to various owners and the lands were divided. Finally, in 1971 the San Bernardino County Board of Supervisors bought the house and an acre of land. The little building was in sad condition, damaged by flooding in 1969.

Vandals had made off with every window, door and fixture. A "march for history" by Cucamonga school children sparked the restoration.

But step inside. The U-shaped house faces south and encloses a little square patio with a round cistern. An open flume once carried a cool canyon stream from the hills, under the kitchen wing, into the cistern (where residents and guests could dip up the water), then under the house to the orchards in front. You'll find a parlor and bedrooms, a winter kitchen and a summer kitchen in one wing, and three guest bedrooms in the other wing.

Under the twelve foot ceilings, the house curators have an array of furniture (around the 1860 time period). The black dresses of Dona Merced and her relatives are elegantly small. Walking shoes for a child seem the size for a doll. Somehow, the life of this surprising house is still close at hand.

How to get there: The Rains House is at 8810 Hemlock St., corner of Vineyard Ave. From the 10 Freeway exit at Vineyard Ave. and drive north to Hemlock. Call (909) 989-4970.

Jedediah Smith Memorial

◇ *San Dimas* ◇

MUD SPRINGS—not a lovely name. More gentle was the early Spanish name for the spot: La Cienega, a wet or marshy place. Today this same area is known as San Dimas.

In November of 1826, a young man led his tattered party of twelve men to camp at Mud Springs. They had traveled from Utah, along the Colorado River and over the Mojave Desert, crossing the San Bernardino Mountains by an Indian route near Cajon Pass, and into the oak-dotted valley. The young pathfinder, aged twenty-seven, was Jedediah Smith.

One of ten children, Smith was born in New York state and set out early to join the hardy "mountain men" exploring the West. They sought the valuable beaver for gentlemen's hats, and opened up many routes used in later settlement. His first expeditions had some hard trials: in the Yellowstone trapping grounds a grizzly seized his head, costing him an eyebrow and almost an ear. Ever the leader, he gave his men instructions while they sewed back the ear.

Thus seasoned, "Diah" became the first American to enter California from the East and later the first to cross the Sierra Nevada Range. His routes covered thousands of miles across the Great Basin and Southwest, up into Northern California and Oregon, past the Smith River named for him. He died in an Indian ambush in New Mexico, on the Santa Fe Trail, at the age of thirty-two.

Smith's journal, now published in paperback, tells us about his route into California in 1826-27 and his stay at Mission San Gabriel. To honor him the San Dimas Festival of Western Arts commissioned a life-sized bronze statue, now outside the City Hall. The sculptor was Victor Issa.

A faint smile animates the statue's face. This was a young man who spent much of his life looking out across terrain he had never seen before. Here he seems to be pleased with the prospect of Mud Springs and the Mission's cattle scattered across ample grasslands.

As you circle the statue, you'll note his fringed garb and the few accoutrements of the mountain men: gun and powderhorn, knife, and pouches for supplies. No wonder he blessed the Mission padres who provided 64 yards of cloth, enough to make a shirt for each of his men.

Not far from the statue is the site of Mud Springs, near the present Arrow Highway. The marker tells that near this place "favored by the Indians," Juan Bautista de Anza had passed in 1774, travelling from Sonora, Mexico, to Monterey, California. In this spot full of memories, you can pay your respects to pathfinders who paused here for the gift of water.

How to get there: The sculpture is at the intersection of Walnut Ave. and Bonita Ave. From the 210 Freeway, exit at Bonita and drive east. The marker is on Arrow Hwy just east of Walnut Ave. Call the San Dimas Historical Society at (909) 592-1190.

San Dimas Railroad Depot
✧ *San Dimas* ✧

RAILROAD DEPOTS in Southern California now have varied uses. Some are Metrolink stations, while others hold community centers, restaurants, or offices. Some house memories of their own past. Others have been whisked out of development's way, down the very highways that once replaced our railways.

The San Dimas Railroad Depot is a fine spot to ponder the history of human mobility. Near this bright yellow station, the Santa Fe drove the "last spike" in completing its Chicago-Los Angeles line in 1887. The little community there was Mud Springs, now the Western-spirited town of San Dimas.

A wooden Victorian train station was built first, but it burned in 1933. The present depot, finished in 1934, neatly combines the styles of Spanish Colonial revival and the Moderne of the 1930s. Its architect, Herbert Gilman, designed most of the Santa Fe stations in the West. The present color, which startled town officials in a recent

restoration, is the original hue—taken from the colors of the Santa Fe railroad (still visible on the freights that slowly rumble through).

The historic train depots were snug and compact, serving their purpose, no nonsense but a dash of style. This one handled passengers until the mid-1950s and freight until 1968. The City of San Dimas bought the building in 1974 and used it for community and senior citizen activities.

Then in 1995, just as other depots were disappearing or precariously holding on, this one was leased to the Pacific Railroad Society (organized 1936) for its museum, library, and archives. The waiting room now holds exhibits, and the luggage and freight rooms are well-stuffed with books, timetables, and maps. Additions to these collections are welcome.

On display is a photograph set of classy little depots. Is your town's depot here? You'll see La Verne, Glendora, Pasadena, Arcadia, Redlands, Palms (this one, rescued, is now at Heritage Square along the Pasadena Freeway) and more. Pacific Railroad Society members were on the last train of the Mount Lowe Railway, running on the Alpine Division in 1937.

A gem of the collection is a big relief map of the Pacific Electric, once the largest electric railway system in the world. It stretched from the ocean "through the Kingdom of the Orange" as far as Redlands. This map of about 1912 shows an overview of Southland geography, wide open spaces with names of villages which have disappeared or now become cities.

Note, too, the photo of an elegant dinner party, tinged with Hollywood glamour, aboard the Santa Fe Super Chief in 1937.

In this sturdy little depot, meet the Pacific Railroad Society, which preserves an 1887 timetable of the first transcontinental passenger trains, but also has a Home Page on the Internet. You can join them for their work parties or their Railfan trips far and wide on the trains of today.

How to get there: The Depot is at 210 W. Bonita Ave., San Dimas. From the 210 Freeway, exit at Arrow Highway, drive east, and turn left on Bonita Ave. For information, call (909) 394-0616.

The Madonna of the Trail
✧ *Upland* ✧

IT RAINED on and off that February day in 1929, but the participants showed the same spirit they were there to celebrate. It was dedication day for the Madonna of the Trail, a monumental sculpture set in Upland's tree-lined Euclid Avenue.

The Madonna is "A Memorial to the Pioneer Mothers of the Covered Wagon Days." She is one of twelve identical statues along a string of old trails that crossed the United States.

In a nationwide effort between 1911 and 1929, the National Old

Trails Road Association and the Daughters of the American Revolution chose a route, including both Indian and pioneer trails. The route follows the National Pike Road, Boone's Lick Road, Washington or Braddock Road, the Cumberland Road, and the Santa Fe Trail from St. Louis to California. Set along the way, the easternmost statue is in Bethesda, Maryland; the westernmost, in Upland.

Tracing this historic route in reverse today, you would take US 40 across Arizona to Albuquerque, US 25 north to US 70, and follow the latter all the way to the East Coast.

August Leimbach, a German sculptor in St. Louis, was commissioned to create the twelve Madonnas, each ten feet tall. He used Algonite Stone, an aggregate based on Missouri granite. He was paid $1,000 for each of the five-ton statues.

A special crane brought in from Los Angeles set the Upland Madonna on her six-foot base, which itself weighed twelve tons. The parkway, bordered with citrus groves, was filled with people as the statue was unveiled by Carolyn Emily Cox, age 81. She had traveled the Santa Fe Trail from Iowa to California by wagon herself as a small child.

The parade that day was on the theme of transportation. Riders on horseback were followed by wagons and stage coaches, and finally the motor cars of 1929, with a little airplane skimming low overhead.

John Steven McGroarty, California's poet laureate and author of the Mission Play that was performed for many years in San Gabriel, gave a speech. Expected but unable to attend was a Missouri judge who was Director of the National Old Trails Road Association: Harry S. Truman.

The base of the statue notes that Jedediah Smith passed along this trail in 1826 with his men, the first Americans to enter California overland. Today, you can see a fine sculpture of him just a few miles west of the Madonna, in front of the San Dimas City Hall.

With a baby on one hip and another child clinging to her skirt, the Madonna of the Trail strides firmly onward. In her right hand is not a walking staff but a long-barreled gun. Her gaze seems to reach far ahead. She is the pioneer mother, who has crossed many miles and can cross more.

How to get there: The Madonna is at the intersection of Foothill Blvd. and Euclid Ave. From the 210 Freeway, continue east on the 30 Freeway to its end at Foothill Blvd., then east to Euclid Ave.

Old San Antonio Hospital
⬦ *Upland* ⬦

SOME BUILDINGS in the Southland seem to have nine lives. They carry on into a new use as easily as a cat landing on its feet. One such building is the Old San Antonio Hospital in Upland.

This Craftsman style structure was built in 1907 on a dirt road known as Arrow. Its lower story was cobblestone and the main level stucco, with stone piers under a three-gable roof. For many years it was the first and only hospital in the Upland/Ontario area. Dr. William Craig had been performing surgery in local homes and he was the main force in getting a real hospital built.

Miss Anna Shaw was the first superintendant of the hospital, which also had a nursing school and trained many young women in the early years. The two-story building held eight private wards, two four-bed wards, and the operating room.

Upland's population was about 1,500 in 1907, but soon a larger hospital was needed and one was built nearby in 1924. The original San Antonio Hospital began a new life as a resort—from 1925-35.

182

The Brethren in Christ Church bought the building in 1935 and established Beulah College there. In 1950 the school was renamed Upland College—another life?—and so it remained until 1965.

The Salvation Army came next to start a training school there, but the building was little used for a decade. Then in 1976 it was sold to the Astara Foundation, the current owner, an educational publisher of spiritual teachings. In 1980 it was listed on the National Register of Historic Places.

The city of Upland had begun as part of Ontario, the "model colony" founded by the brothers George and W.B. Chaffey from Ontario, Canada in 1882. Five years later the Bedford brothers purchased the north section and planned a town called Magnolia. In 1902 they re-named their town site Upland.

Its 200-foot wide Euclid Avenue, lined with tall trees, stretched toward the mountains. River stones were used in curbs, bridges, and walls. Many of these remain today in the city as do scattered fruit trees from the early days.

Upland's historic chronology includes: 1885, Santa Fe Railroad completed through the town; 1893, the Upland Lemon Growers organized; 1895 or 96, mule car trolley converted to electric trolleys. Two newspapers started, schools and churches, a women's club (1903)…The chronology is punctuated with years of bad freezes or floods, right up to the 1970s.

Through this, the hospital building carried on. Today it still looks at home on Arrow Highway, keeping up its mission of health and teaching. Inside and out, it is little changed.

How to get there: The old hospital is at 792 W. Arrow Highway. From the 10 Freeway exit at Euclid Ave. and drive north. Turn left at Arrow.

Alex Theater - Glendale California

The Eagle Rock
◇ *Eagle Rock* ◇

WHERE DID IT come from, that beaky monolith and well-loved landmark of the San Rafael Hills known as Eagle Rock? That's a long story.

About 10 to 15 million years long, according to a recent paper by geologist Guiseppe Cugno. The earliest millenia of the rock went something like this: a mixture of sand, gravel, and rocky cobbles was deposited in a watery environment. Fish fossils in the bedrock show evidence of the age. Geologic conditions eventually fused the deposits.

Then tectonic forces, which cause the continental plates to slip and sometimes collide, uplifted the Eagle Rock and the hills to the south. Finally, erosion and spalling, or natural chipping, carved the mysterious form on the west side of the rounded rock.

The same rock formations can be seen along Figueroa Blvd. and in the hills south of the Eagle Rock Plaza, but none is as large and visible as the landmark itself.

Human history came later. The Native Americans called Gabrielinos had a village at springs in the canyon below the rock. By the 1870s the Rancho San Rafael was being divided and settlers were arriving. Soon herds of sheep grazed on the broad plain, while swallows were nesting in the two deep hollows at the base of the rock.

Those same hollows had been occupied by the famed bandit Tiburcio Vasquez in the days before his final robbery and capture in 1874.

A generation later the *Los Angeles Herald* wrote in 1909 of "the pretty little suburb of Eagle Rock...awakened into life by the magic wand of Huntington's Trolley System." Although just six miles from Los Angeles, the valley was "a picturesque bit of country scenery," busy with truck gardens, orchards and the famous Gates strawberry farm. A country wagon road bisected the valley from west to east, connecting Glendale with Pasadena. The rock was visible for many miles in the rural landscape.

Easter sunrise services have been held at the rock, and some members of the Eagle Rock Valley Historical Society remember a cross growing there made of silvery dusty miller plants. Long-time residents say the best time of year to see the eagle most sharply is in June or July, about 3 p.m. The image is either an eagle with full wingspread, half released from its rock captivity—or just the beak of a huge eagle head. It all depends on the shadows and the eye of the beholder.

In 1923 the town of Eagle Rock agreed to be annexed by the city of Los Angeles, to provide much needed water and a high school. But the rock still marks the identity of an early Southern California community. Several years ago, to avert construction of apartments nearby, the City of Los Angeles purchased the rock and 2.5 acres of surrounding land. Today the eagle still flies free.

How to get there: For information and exhibits, contact the Eagle Rock Valley Historical Society, (323) 257-0524.

Women's Twentieth Century Club
◇ *Eagle Rock* ◇

WOMEN HAVE BEEN called "the makers and menders of the social fabric." In the early years of many Southern California towns, women formed clubs for friendship and to strengthen their communities. In Eagle Rock, at almost one hundred years old, the Women's Twentieth Century Club still occupies its classic Craftsman-style clubhouse on Colorado Boulevard.

In 1903, several hundred settlers occupied farms and a town center in the Eagle Rock Valley. Strawberries and citrus thrived under the watchful beak of the Rock, already a landmark known far and wide. In that year, eleven women met in Mrs. Philip Parker's home to found a club, named for the new century. Its motto would be "Knowledge is Power," and its mission: education and service.

With some materials and work donated, the Club members laid the cornerstone of their clubhouse in 1914. By selling subscriptions to the *Los Angeles Times*, members acquired 150 sets of the dishes the newspaper was giving as premiums. The Hamburger Department Store (now the May Company) subsidized the furnishings.

The shingled clubhouse, still a rich redwood brown, is a Los Angeles Cultural Heritage Monument and one of the few large-scale Craftsman buildings left in Southern California. The building is tall, but its hipped roof gives the effect of sheltering the large space within. A miniature hipped roof shades the entrance. Pines and magnolias cluster near the front porch. To the north, French doors open onto a veranda, and a nearby caretaker's cottage (1921) echoes the architecture.

Inside, the main hall resembles a stylish barn, rising two stories and lighted with high bands of windows. It seats 250 for meetings and dinners. The foyer, with its brick fireplace, is popular for weddings.

The activities held in this unusual building trace the social history of the town. This was one of the first Women's Clubs to sign a petition supporting Women's Suffrage. They led in the war effort of both World Wars, and established a site for the local Carnegie Library. They organized the Eagle Rock Valley Historical Society, and maintained a well-baby clinic in this Clubhouse for thirty-five years.

Their philanthropic projects have included Save the Redwoods, scholarships, construction of the Eagle Rock Bowl (now the amphitheater at Occidental College) and other community efforts.

Always strong for California history and natural beauty, the members hosted John Steven McGroarty (author of the famed Mission Play) and Gene Stratton Porter (the naturalist and novelist) for lectures here. Also speaking was Mrs. Valley Knudsen, an advocate of civic beautification whose little Victorian home is now at Heritage Square beside the Pasadena Freeway.

The Twentieth Century Women's Club has evolved with its century and approaches the new one with optimism. Meanwhile, its historic building belongs to both past and present in the Eagle Rock Valley.

How to get there: The Clubhouse is at 5105 Hermosa Ave., corner of Colorado Blvd. From the 134 Freeway, exit at Colorado and drive west. For information, call (323) 256-9512.

Early Buildings of Occidental College
◇ *Eagle Rock* ◇

LIFE WAS GETTING hectic there in Highland Park for the little college. Its site, once peaceful, was bothered by streetcar lines and even cut by a transcontinental railroad. In 1912, it was time to move on.

The school was already something of a gypsy. In 1887 a committee of Presbyterian ministers had established it as The Occidental University of Los Angeles ("for Boarding and Day Pupils. Both Sexes") on 50 acres just east of the L.A. city limits. 27 men and 13 women enrolled. But the next year the local land boom collapsed and in 1891 only six students came, two graduating in 1893.

Fire destroyed the school's Boyle Heights building in 1896, so Occidental College (its revised name) rented rooms for two years on Hill Street between 6th and 7th in downtown Los Angeles.

Highland Park seemed ideal in 1898, as the college moved its 15 students into the farmlands by the Arroyo Seco, settling at Figueroa and Avenue 50. Three brick buildings were erected there, one still

standing today. Teddy Roosevelt visited the school with his friend Charles Lummis in 1911, and students gave him a round of "Harvard yells".

The next year, Occidental College acquired its present home in the Eagle Rock Valley, by purchase and gift. The region had been the 36,000 acre Rancho San Rafael of Don Jose Maria Verdugo. Chaparral slopes edged a quilt of orchards, vineyards, and melon fields below the landmark rock.

Early photographs show the rural setting, but the topography was a problem. Terracing was needed to plant the young college into its hillside spot.

Noted architect Myron Hunt drew up the campus plans, which were to become a major interest of his life. He designed a total of 21 buildings for Occidental, up to the year 1944. The original three were the Johnson Hall of Letters, Fowler Hall of Science, and James Swan Hall as a men's dormitory. Excavating for Johnson, workmen found a large underground spring and considered abandoning the site. Similar springs also appeared under later hillside buildings.

Just before the move, Pomona College Trustees had proposed merging the two schools, but Occidental declined. In 1912 "Oxy" refused its Trustees' proposal to become "men only," and 1914 saw the first graduation on the new campus.

The college catalogue of that year describes Myron Hunt's three buildings as Italian Renaissance style, of reinforced concrete and white stucco. All were "strictly fireproof." A broad staircase rose to the upper two (Johnson and Fowler), which held class rooms, a chapel, library, post office, cafe, bookstore, and administration. A YWCA was in one, a YMCA in the other. Swan Hall had sleeping balconies and rooms at $45 per semester. (The women students were housed in nearby "reputable homes.")

Myron Hunt added nine more buildings in the 1920s, including the Hillside Theater and Freeman Union. Clearly, this was home now. The gypsy youth of Occidental College was over.

How to get there: The College is at 1600 Campus Road. For directions, call (323) 259-2500.

Eagle Rock Community Cultural Center

⬦ *Eagle Rock* ⬦

RAINSTICKS, CLAY WHISTLES, and rain forest water drums—in a library?

Well, yes and no. For this handsome Spanish gothic building in Eagle Rock, scene of music on handmade instruments from South America and Mexico, is no longer a library. Near its door, a bookdrop marked "Books" remains just for memories, but this is now the Eagle Rock Community Cultural Center.

Its story begins in 1914, when residents of Eagle Rock (then an independent town) aspired to have a real library. Before that date, Miss Anna Swan had checked out books to residents one day a week from her dry goods store. But W. L. Miller, editor of the "Eagle Rock Sentinel" felt their town worthy of having a Carnegie library.

Miller recruited the Women's Twentieth Century Club (still a local landmark) and the school P.T.A. to promote the cause. The steel

magnate Andrew Carnegie was taking requests from cities and towns for new libraries. Eventually he established about 2800 across America. (The city of Los Angeles had ten, of which four remain today: Cahuenga, Lincoln Heights, Vermont Square and Eagle Rock).

In 1914 the Carnegie trustees granted $7,500 for Eagle Rock's new library. It opened in 1915 with a "book party" and the contribution of hundreds of books. In 1923, Eagle Rock became part of the city of Los Angeles and thereafter the library was a branch of the Los Angeles Public Library.

A new and larger building, on the same foundation, replaced the original Carnegie library in 1927 and this is the structure you see today. Its architects, Henry C. Newton and Robert D. Murray, preserved the original style but increased the book capacity.

But finally the city closed the historic library and built another one nearby. It was a precarious time for the old landmark, which goes back to the days of Eagle Rock's independence. What would be its fate?

Citizen spirit eventually saved the day, and the building was listed on the National Register of Historic Places. Several years ago, beautifully restored, it opened as the Eagle Rock Community Cultural Center (a partnership between the city and an independent association). The building contains a large brightly-windowed hall for performances and events, plus exhibition space, class rooms and offices. Gothic arches, bookshelves, and coppery light fixtures give the aura of a library, but the new uses fit right in.

Now about those clay whistles and shells that sound like frogs: check with the staff for free family workshops like the recent "Instruments from the Ancient Americas".

Also on the Center's agenda are art classes for children (age 6-12) including painting, dance, photography, and more. An Electronic Arts Academy (computer graphics), art exhibits, and street festivals have been planned. Andrew Carnegie might be amazed but pleased at such doings.

How to get there: The Center is at 2225 Colorado Blvd. From the 134 Freeway, exit at Colorado Blvd. and drive west. Telephone (323) 226-1617.

Doctors' House

✧ *Glendale* ✧

IF ARCHITECTURE has a vocabulary, then the Doctors' House in Glendale has quite a lot to say.

The two-story wood frame home was built in the late 1880's and first sold in 1890 for $1,500 cash. Later a series of four doctors occupied the house (three physicians and a chemist), eventually giving the house its name.

In its architectural detail the house speaks several languages. It shows Queen Anne /Eastlake style in its silhouette, with a square tower, gables, porches, and curving shapes. Another language is the stick style, which uses stick trims in various patterns.

The exterior today seems to chatter amiably with this decorative and structural "vocabulary." Three moongate-arch porches lighten the first story, providing indoor-outdoor spaces.

Another unusual feature is the Gibb doors, which are actually double-hung windows reaching to the porch floors. By lifting the lower part, one can make a "doorway" and step out—or the upper sash can be lowered like a window to provide air.

This home was originally at Wilson and Belmont streets. There Dr. Charles Bogue, physician to the Verdugo family, lived beginning in 1895. Dr. David Hunt, who was said to have owned Glendale's first automobile, bought the property and Dr. Bogue's practice in 1901.

By 1907, Dr. Allen Bryant, who obtained Carnegie support for the city's first library, lived in the house. Finally, Dr. Leonidas Hurtt, a chemist who was first president of the Glendale Chamber of Commerce, moved in and added some lemon and orange groves.

Each of these families was important to Glendale's progress. Their efforts ranged from the Tuesday Afternoon Club (the city's first philanthropic group, founded by Nellie Bogue) to service on school boards and bringing the Pacific Electric Line into the city.

In 1980 the doctors were gone, but later owners had changed the home very little. The Doctors' House was in the path of development but the patient was strong enough to stand an operation.

Thanks to the Glendale Historical Society and local businesses, the house was bought and moved by night to its present site beside the Brand Library. More than 150 volunteers contributed over 18,000 total hours of restoration—working Saturdays for three years.

Today the inside of the house looks alive. Docents often arrange a continuous theme throughout the house: a wedding, or Christmas decorations. Objects from the occupants' daily lives are scattered casually about.

Don't miss the Wooten desk, solid oak with 103 compartments, in the doctor's office. President Grant and Queen Victoria each had one, and we're told there is a society for owners of such desks. In several rooms, wallpaper has been replicated from original scraps. In the kitchen is an unusual iron stove, a domestic work of art.

How to get there: The Doctors' House is at 1601 W. Mountain Street (in Brand Park). From the 134 Freeway, exit at Pacific Ave., drive north to Kenneth Rd., then left to Grandview Ave. and right to the park entrance. Call the Glendale Historical Society at (818) 242-7447.

Miss American Green Cross
✧ *Glendale* ✧

FROM ACCLAIM TO OBLIVION and part way back—it seems like a poignant fate for a lady. And a lady with a mission, at that.

Her glory days were in 1928, when she was created and unveiled in a ceremony attended by thousands. Today Miss American Green Cross, returned to obscure dignity, stands behind Glendale's Brand Library at the foot of the Verdugo Hills.

The Green Cross was an early organization devoted to saving America's forests. Records from 1930 show their offices were in the Bradbury Building in downtown Los Angeles. In 1928 the first local chapter was established in Glendale, and the statue was dedicated on May 23 that year.

A bronze female figure, in classical garb and laurel wreath, stands against a green cross reminiscent of the healing powers of the Red Cross. Across her brow a band reads "America." At her feet is a jumble of broken logs, showing forest destruction. Her arms are outstretched in a plea for awareness. The effect is something like a crucifix, or a ship's figurehead.

On the base is the message: "Help save our trees." And "The forest is the mother of the rivers." Sculptor of the 18-foot monument was Frederick Willard Potter. Miss Verlyn Sumner was the model, appearing with the statue in early photographs.

At the dedication, more than 100 cars accompanied California Governor C.C. Young and other dignitaries to the statue's site at the old Glendale High School, Broadway and Verdugo Road. 4,000 school children took part, one placing a copper box of mementos into the pedestal.

The numerous speakers included Count Ilya Tolstoy, telling of reforestation in Europe. Newsreel companies covered the event, and photos of the unveiling were carried in rotogravure sections of newspapers in more than 40 cities.

Green Cross members believed that extensive tree planting would create a wetter climate in Southern California, and would provide natural flood control. Spirits were high on that May day. "Glendale has done a fine thing for the nation," said Governor Young.

But the budding movement waned in the 1930s. Perhaps the economic woes of the Depression distracted public concern. The worst indignity: the monument was struck by a car from a nearby collision in 1934. At some point the park superintendent moved the lady and her pedestal to a hollow in the Verdugo foothills.

There she languished, her arms broken away by vandals and the elements until she was rediscovered by hikers in the 1950s and put in protective storage. She was restored by local architect Ron Pekar, using only original materials. Latex molds were made to recreate the cement logs. A new unveiling of the monument was held in September 1992, and today it seems her message was right, after all.

How to get there: Brand Park is at 1601 W. Mountain St., at the end of Grandview Ave. From the 134 Freeway, exit at Central Ave., drive north, left on Glenoaks Blvd. and right on Grandview. Contact the Glendale Historical Society at (818) 242-7447.

Casa Adobe de San Rafael
✧ *Glendale* ✧

ANY SOUTHERN CALIFORNIA building with a pedigree from the Verdugo and Sepulveda families, not to mention the colorful lawman Tomas Sanchez, attracts our attention.

The house is in Glendale and now called the Casa Adobe de San Rafael. Sanchez, sheriff of Los Angeles County from 1859 to 1867, built the adobe around 1870 and settled there with his wife Maria Sepulveda de Sanchez. One hundred acres of Jose Verdugo's Rancho San Rafael had been deeded to them by Rafaela Verdugo, who was Maria's stepmother and a granddaughter of Jose Verdugo.

Their land was part of the 36,000 acre Verdugo property, once covering part or all of present Glendale, Burbank, Eagle Rock, Highland Park, La Canada Flintridge, Montrose, and Pasadena. Boundaries were the Arroyo Seco on the East and South, the Los Angeles River on the West, and the Sierra Madre (now San Gabriel) Mountains on the North.

Tomas had married Maria when she was thirteen years old, and they had nineteen sons and two daughters. A third generation Californian, Sanchez captured some early outlaws and was named Judge of the Plains by the U.S. Government.

Sanchez built a simple rectangular home, one-story, with outdoor verandas on the south and west. Originally a lean-to kitchen served for cooking. The "sala" or formal main room, was 34 x 16 feet in size. The other three rooms were a family dining room and two bedrooms.

The 18-inch thick walls supported an early California belief that adobes are the coolest, the warmest, the cheapest, and most earthquake-proof houses, and the best houses for fandangos.

Sanchez died in 1882 and Maria survived him by thirty years. But debt forced her to sell her home in 1883 for $12,000 to Andrew Glassell. Within a decade, the property changed hands ten times and was frequently divided in the land boom of the 1880s.

All seemed over for the old adobe in 1930, when its then owner, California Medicinal Wine Co., planned to remove the house and its old trees for a subdivision. To the rescue came civic groups including the American Green Cross, which worked for preservation of trees. To raise funds, a fiesta was held in June 1930 at the adobe. 400 people in Spanish California costume danced and heard talks on local history and reforestation. John Steven McGroarty, author of the famed Mission Play, was the main speaker, and he brought dancers from his play's cast.

In 1932 the City of Glendale bought the adobe and two acres for a park. Restoration provided employment in the Depression, through the State Emergency Relief Administration.

At the Casa Adobe you can enjoy a picnic under the wisteria arbor, then step inside to see vintage furniture, curious old tools, and a rose-painted mirror once owned by Governor Pio Pico.

How to get there: Casa Adobe de San Rafael is at 1330 Dorothy Drive. From the 134 Freeway, exit at Brand Ave., drive north, turn left on Stocker St. and right on Dorothy Dr. Call the Glendale Historical Society at (818) 242-7447.

Brand Library

◇ *Glendale* ◇

IT ALL BEGAN with the 1893 Columbian World Exposition in Chicago. There the East Indian Pavilion, with its Islamic-style grace, struck a spark which eventually landed in Glendale, California.

The fascinated visitor to the fair was Leslie C. Brand, a native of St. Louis. Brand had come to California in 1886 and set up the Title Guarantee and Trust Company. In partnership with Henry Huntington, he brought prospective land buyers out to Glendale in the red electric cars, to see his real estate developments. Twice a week his ad ran in Los Angeles newspapers: "Have You Been to Glendale?"

For his own home at the foot of the Verdugo Mountains, Brand asked his brother-in-law, Nathaniel Dryden, to recreate the Saracen-styled pavilion he remembered. The cool white mansion set in terraces of lawns was a fantasy of domes, minarets, and scalloped arches. It seemed like a Moorish palace, backed by chaparral-covered California hillsides. The home was finished in 1904 and named El Miradero: the place with a view.

The 10-room interior was thoroughly Victorian, with mahogany and oak woodwork, Tiffany glass, stencilled ceilings, arched doorways and fretwork carvings. The rooms opened on a central glass-domed solarium.

Brand lived with dash and style. A landing strip and Moorish-styled aerodrome handled his fleet of planes, including French and German war planes. He hired pilots to "fly-in" celebrities and movie stars for his parties. He enjoyed fabulous autos too and owned a Packard and a Duesenberg, among others.

From 1902 to 1925, Brand actively developed northern Glendale. He eventually owned about 20,000 acres and also telephone, water, and power companies in the area. A shrewd businessman, he helped to finance such landmarks as the Masonic Temple, the Elks Lodge, and the Tuesday Afternoon Club.

When he died in 1925, he deeded 488 acres of his land to the city of Glendale for a public park, providing his wife could live there until her death (which was in 1945).

In 1956, the Glendale Public Library opened a branch in the Saracen palace. The great fireplace in the entrance hall, the tracery of the windows, remain to this day.

Now shelves of books, records, and slides fill the mansion. Leaded glass windows and Italian tiles make a choice setting for the collections, all in art and music. The Moorish folly has become a gem of a library.

An adjacent building, completed in 1969, holds a gallery, concert hall, and studios for city art programs. About 21,000 square feet of space were added to the 5,000 square feet of the house.

The surroundings today are a pleasant park, ideal for picnics and children's play. Approaching from the south, you'll enter a turreted gateway, then pass along a palm-lined drive. Just ahead is the Moorish fantasy, full of books, a memory from a long ago world's fair.

How to get there: From the 134 Freeway, exit at Central Ave. and drive north, turn left on Kenneth Rd. and right on Grandview Av. to its end at the park entrance. For information, call (818) 548-2051.#

Verdugo Adobe
✧ *Glendale* ✧

VERDUGO CANYON winds in a north and south direction, a green cleft between the San Rafael Hills on the east and the Verdugo Hills on the west. Years ago the canyon was surely a waterway; today the 2 Freeway winds along its hillsides toward the Los Angeles Basin below.

These lands were once held by Jose Maria Verdugo, who was granted a grazing permit there in 1784 by the Spanish governor of California. This property of about 36,000 acres was known as the Rancho San Rafael and was bequeathed to two of Jose Maria's children, Julio and Catalina, when he died in 1831. Originally the rancho included part of present day Glendale, Burbank, Highland Park, the Eagle Rock valley, and Pasadena west of the Arroyo Seco.

Land claims had to be renegotiated when California was ceded to the United States by Mexico in 1846. Subdivisions and ownership changes continued into the twentieth century. But after all this, the little adobe house of the Verdugos is still in its spot, there in the green canyon.

Accounts differ about when the adobe was built. Some sources hold that Don Jose Maria Verdugo built it for his daughter Catalina, in 1828. Other historians accept that Teodoro Verdugo, son of Julio, constructed the adobe in the 1860s.

The house remained in private ownership for many decades. Fortunately the residents knew its historical importance and preserved it well. Originally its single-story contained two rooms, with adobe walls about 24 inches thick and a long veranda facing east. Later owners added a simple kitchen, bathroom and another room, all of wood frame construction.

The adobe's last owners were Dr. and Mrs. Ernest Bashor. Their heirs sold the house and its remaining gardens to the City of Glendale in 1989. Today it is used by the Department of Parks and Recreation as park ranger offices.

All is quiet now at the Verdugo Adobe. Traffic on nearby residential streets seems distant. A steep hill rises just behind the old house and the grounds are densely shaded with various trees. Early photographs show the adobe in more open surroundings, with views across the grassy canyon.

Still on the property are the remains of a historic tree, called the "oak of peace." A marker indicates that there General Andres Pico met envoys of General John C. Fremont, to plan the Treaty of Cahuenga which ended the war of Mexico and the U.S. in 1847. The ancient tree has fallen, but just up the slope is another monumental oak of equal dignity. This is a pleasant little park to sit a while and contemplate the layers of our past, perhaps with a favorite history book in hand.

How to get there: The adobe is at 2211 Bonita Drive in Glendale. From the 2 Freeway, exit at Mountain St. and drive west. Turn right on Verdugo Blvd., then left on Opechee Way and left on Bonita. Call (818) 548-3795.

Alex Theatre
✧ Glendale ✧

HAVE YOU EVER been in an "atmospherium?" That's the name for an indoor space with the illusion of open air—like the blue twilight of an enclosed garden. You'll find one at the Alex Theatre in Glendale.

Known as the Alexander at first, it was completed in 1925 as a vaudeville and movie house. Architects Charles Selkirk and Arthur Lindley designed a rich blend of Greek and Egyptian ideas: columns, friezes, bamboos, palms, and plenty of gold. The open forecourt was, and still is, a beguiling entrance. It was the era of such palaces;

Grauman's Egyptian Theatre had opened in Hollywood just a year before.

The Alexander was named for a three-year-old: the son of theater magnate Claude Langley. The grand opening featured the world premiere of an eight-reel silent film "Lightnin", organ music, and eight acts of vaudeville. Two perfomances each drew over 2000 people.

The first talking picture at the Alexander ran in 1929. For the next two decades, the

204

theatre thrived on first run films and glamorous stars. The list of previews there looks like film history. Elizabeth Taylor and her mother came in 1944 for "National Velvet", and that same year Bing Crosby attended the preview of "Going My Way."

There were stranger happenings at the Alexander too. In 1938, about 5,000 Glendale women attended demonstrations of gas cooking there, sponsored by the local gas company to show that such cookery was safe and easy. Many of our vintage buildings had a special role in wartime: at the Alexander it was war bond rallies during World War II.

In 1940 remodeling added the 100-foot obelisk, with its glowing neon and a spiky star at the top. Also in S. Charles Lee's design was the three-dimensional marquee. Along with this Art Deco flavor, Lee told Fox Theaters president Spyros Skouras that the long name "would have to go": it didn't suit the neon. Thereafter, it would be the "Alex".

A backstage fire struck the Alex in 1948, and this time the redecorators got to the interior. Restoration included lots of satin and velvet swags, draped here and there. Even the fluted columns at each side of the stage were covered with pleated fabric.

From "Ben Hur" to "Star Wars", the Alex carried on with the blockbusters of the moment. Wide-screen Cinemascope caused excitement in the 1950s. But after the 1960s the balcony was closed, due to smaller audiences.

Then, the theater went dark in the early 1990s, its fate in doubt. Purchased by the Glendale Redevelopment Agency, it is now restored to its original style and is a beautiful venue (no more velvet swags) for music, dance, and films.

Stepping into the balcony, you're once again in the twilight—or is it dawn?—of an Egyptian garden, at the Alex.

How to get there: The Alex is at 216 N. Brand Blvd. From the 134 Freeway, exit at Brand and drive south. For ticket information, call 1-800-233-3123.

Entrance Tunnel, Southwest Museum
✧ *Highland Park* ✧

WHICH OF US has not looked sometimes for the light at the end of the tunnel?

Have this experience for yourself at the historic tunnel entrance to the Southwest Museum in Highland Park. The landmark museum building, perched so visibly above the Pasadena Freeway, was originally reached through a tunnel into Mt. Washington. The tunnel and elevator were opened in March 1920, taking visitors up to the Mission Revival-style museum and its seven-story tower. Shown there are world-class collections of Native American art and culture. The enterprise was founded by the colorful Charles Lummis and his Southwest Society for archaeology and ethnology.

The tunnel is 240 feet long, ten feet high, and eight feet wide. At its entrance is a Mayan-style facade, made of concrete with carved panels. Deep inside the hill, visitors step into an elevator and are whisked up to a tall, light-filled lobby of the building.

But the tunnel, fondly re-membered by many Southern Californians, was closed for many years. Earthquakes and rains had taken their toll. The old elevator was a relic in itself. Much restoration was needed before the tunnel's re-opening celebration in 1996.

Best of all, the 20 dioramas of Native American scenes, set into the walls of the tunnel, can now be seen again. Originally called "the habitat groups," they show daily activities of the people whose cultures appear in the museum above. The miniature panoramas were made between 1919 and 1930 by Elizabeth Mason of Santa Barbara.

Which is your favorite? In one mini-drama, a bear impersonator terrifies Pomo women who shy away from the shaman's power with fascinated respect. In a night scene of the Gabrielino settlement Yangna, a man holds up a glowing torch. These dioramas draw you into the past, and into the spirit-world.

Others show the famed sites of Chichen Itza, Machu Picchu, and the Mayan temple of Palenque. Dwellings include pueblos of Mesa Verde, a Hopi interior, and Inuit houses of the far north, shaped by driftwood or whale ribs and partly underground.

The painted background landscapes blend seamlessly with the plants and figures in front. You'll see that these peoples lived in the open air, a life on the land.

Up in the museum, you'll find other dioramas here and there. These date from 1927-41, and some were made through the Federal Art Project, a branch of President F. D. Roosevelt's Work Projects Administration (WPA) in Depression times.

After you explore the museum, return the way you came. If it's a sunny day, you'll step from the elevator into the arching dimness and there it is: a vibrant glow in the distance, edged with green leaves—it's the light at the end of the tunnel.

How to get there: The Southwest Museum is at 234 Museum Drive in Los Angeles. From the 110 Freeway, exit at Avenue 43 and follow the signs directing to the museum. To enter the tunnel, park below, not in the hilltop parking. Call (323) 221-2164.

El Alisal (the Lummis Home)
✧ *Highland Park* ✧

"YOUR HOUSE," wrote a friend to Charles F. Lummis, is "the most novel and characterful and telling in every way of all I have seen this side [of] the continent." The friend was John Muir, and the house was El Alisal, a stone "castle" beside the Arroyo Seco in Highland Park.

Lummis was born in Massachusetts in 1859 and classically educated at Harvard. After a spell of newspaper work in Ohio, young Lummis decided to go to Los Angeles—and that he would walk there. The publisher of the *Los Angeles Daily Times* agreed to publish a weekly dispatch as he trekked and to hire him when he arrived.

So Lummis, aged 25, left Cincinnati in 1884 and walked about 3500 hundred miles in 143 days. So he tells us in his book *A Tramp Across the Continent*. He was welcomed by the Times as "that plucky pedestrian."

Later Lummis also became City Librarian of Los Angeles, then photographed and wrote about much of the Southwest. He orga-

nized the Sequoya Leage to aid the Indians and the Landmarks Club to restore California's neglected missions.

As editor of the magazine *Land of Sunshine* (renamed *Out West* in 1902), Lummis was a crusading voice for Southwestern culture. He published such artists and authors as Mary Austin, Maynard Dixon, and his friend John Muir.

In 1895 Lummis bought three brush-covered acres in a settlement called Garvanza (today known as Highland Park, although the historic name is again on local signs). A fine sycamore tree gave the site its name, El Alisal. He built his own L-shaped house of concrete faced with arroyo stones, its circular stone tower rising to thirty feet. He crafted massive woodwork by hand and added decorative ironwork.

The first room built was the "museo," a long exhibit hall and living room to display artifacts and paintings from his Southwestern travels. The windows are still bordered with black and white photographic transparencies of Indian life, which he took between 1888 and 1896.

In his tower study, known as The Lion's Den, Lummis wrote his books at two desks. From there he could see on a nearby ridge the Southwest Museum, which he had established to house his own and other collections of Indian objects.

His home was lively, with spirited entertainments the host called "Noises." After Lummis died in 1928, family members lived there until 1961. But the house faced an uncertain future as title passed from the Southwest Museum, to the State of California, and finally to the city of Los Angeles in 1971. Now open to visitors, El Alisal is home to the Historical Society of Southern California. There you will find books and other links to much of our colorful regional history. This one-of-a-kind house is surrounded by a native plant garden which is a pleasure in any season.

How to get there: El Alisal is at 200 E. Avenue 43 in Los Angeles. From the 110 Freeway, exit at Avenue 43 and drive northwest. Call (323) 222-0546.

Mount Washington Hotel
✧ *Highland Park* ✧

WHO WERE FLORENCE AND VIRGINIA, and why were they running up and down a Los Angeles hillside all day?

Actually, they were just a small, though intriguing, part of our story, which begins—like many Southern California stories—with the arrival of a young man from the midwest. Robert Marsh was just fourteen years old when he came west from Illinois, first to San Diego, then to Los Angeles.

While still in his twenties, he formed a real estate company which soon took off nicely.

One of his best finds was a 1,000-foot hilltop adjacent to downtown Los Angeles, with views to the sea and to the San Gabriel Mountains. He and his partner Arthur St. Clair Perry bought the summit, fringed by California native walnut trees.

A fine venture, but how to get his clients to the top? The nearby Mt. Lowe Railway was thriving above Pasadena, and Marsh recalled the cog railway on Mt. Washington in New Hampshire. So the part-

ners established the Los Angeles and Mt. Washington Railway, and in 1909 it began taking potential new residents to the heights.

Three funicular railways were eventually built within the Los Angeles City limits, and this one was the longest at 2,900 feet. Marsh's little daughter Florence and Perry's daughter Virginia must have been tickled to have the two cars named for them.

The ticket station at the bottom still stands on Avenue 43 and Marmion Way, now a residence and a city Historic Cultural Monument. The terminal at the top is still there too, near Marsh's next big project, the Mount Washington Hotel.

This three story structure was completed in 1910. Its scale is rather grand for just 18 guest rooms. The film industry was active then in Highland Park, just below the hotel, and for a while the hilltop was busy with movie people and social gatherings.

But by 1919, film-making had shifted to Hollywood. The hotel had outlasted its original purpose in Marsh's real estate development. That year the hotel closed and with it the railway: just ten short years for Florence and Virginia.

How does a large, once-handsome building make it through years of change and survive to the present day? Luck, mainly. The old Mount Washington Hotel was vacant for a time, then served as a military school and then a sanitarium for health seekers.

Then in 1925 Paramahansa Yogananda acquired the property to be the international headquarters of his Self-Realization Fellowship, which it remains to this day. The main building and its grounds can be visited, and they hold some delightful surprises among tall old cedar trees. Outdoor meditation spots include a Temple of Leaves, and Japanese-flavored gardens of gravel paths, little red maples, and ponds.

Your afternoon walk may take you out beyond these grounds too, to sample the hilltop flavor of Mt. Washington.

How to get there: The property is at 3880 San Rafael Avenue, at the corner of Elyria. Consult your Thomas Guide or call for directions and times: (323) 225-2471.

Judson Studios
✧ *Highland Park* ✧

"ART IS ONLY the beautiful way of doing things." With this philosophy, William Lees Judson lived his lifetime as a painter and college dean. Later his family, down to the fifth generation, would operate the distinguished stained glass workshop called the Judson Studios of Southern California.

W. L. Judson was born in Manchester, England, in 1842 and then grew up in Canada. His father and grandfather had been artists, so the family has an unbroken history of two hundred years in this calling, to the present day. Judson settled in Los Angeles in 1893 for his health and soon began painting California landscapes.

He became the first dean of the University of Southern California's College of Fine Arts, established in 1901 in Garvanza (now part of Highland Park) on the Arroyo Seco. The new college was built above the tree-shaded stream. Later the building was enlarged to add the newly organized Arroyo Guild, craftsmen dedicated to high thinking and beautiful handwork.

A fire destroyed that building in 1910, but the present Judson Studios building was begun right away, designed by members of the

Arroyo Guild. It is made of cobblestones, frame, and plaster over metal lath. The rambling front has varied doorways and angles, a small round tower, and cast-stone decorations.

The University took its fine arts classes back to the main campus in 1920, but the Judson Art Glass Company occupied the streamside building. It continues work there to this day. Commissions for stained glass windows have come from many historic California churches and from designers like Frank Lloyd Wright.

In 1913 the Judsons made a huge domed skylight for the Natural History Museum of Los Angeles County (recently cleaned at today's Judson Studios.) The Air Force Academy Chapel in Colorado, a building resembling a giant paper airplane, has glowing windows by the Judson craftsmen.

In 1969, the family was alarmed when their studio building was declared a non-conforming use in its now-residential neighborhood. The structure was saved when the City of Los Angeles named it a historic monument.

Soon after, the Judson Studios proved themselves good neighbors when a fire destroyed five nearby homes, and the Judsons offered temporary housing to a family with eight children.

Earlier, the Arroyo Seco Forum, a kind of artistic "town meeting," was held by the Judsons for almost thirty years. As many as 200 people would attend the programs and addresses, including botanist Theodore Payne and author George Wharton James. The Judson Studios still maintain a welcome place in their neighborhood.

Artists and families lived by mottoes in years past. At the Judson Studios, craftsmen working with the beautiful glass still quote the founder's words: "Only the best is worthwhile."

How to get there: The Judson Studios are at 200 S. Avenue 66, Los Angeles. This is a working studio, so please make arrangements ahead if you would like to visit. For information and directions, call (323) 255-0131.

Oaks of Descanso Gardens
✧ *La Canada Flintridge* ✧

ON OUR WARM DAYS of spring, summer or fall, how to keep
cool while in search of history? Why not follow the English poet
Andrew Marvell, who looked for "a green thought in a green shade?"
There's no better place for this than the forests of Descanso Gardens
in La Canada Flintridge.

In the August dog days, we seek the shade—pools of the deep shad-
owy stuff, or the lighter moods of partial shade. Descanso has a 25
acre native oak forest, a haven for summer walks, and restorative
anytime.

This broad hollow in the San Rafael hills, now part of La Canada
Flintridge, once belonged to Corporal Jose Maria Verdugo. It was
part of a 36,000 acre rancho given to him in 1784 by California's
first Spanish Governor. The Verdugo family held the lands until 1869.

Eventually 165 acres were purchased in 1937 by E. Manchester
Boddy, publisher of the *Los Angeles Daily News*. At that time, the
property had never been developed. It contained oak woodlands

fringed by chaparral on the sunny hills above. Boddy raised camellias under the oak canopies and named his estate the Rancho del Descanso—a place of rest, in Spanish.

Soon he had a thriving flower business and wholesale camellia nursery there. On the hillside he built the family home, today called Hospitality House. Later he added a rose collection and unusual lilacs to the gardens. In 1953, Boddy sold the property to Los Angeles County and spent the rest of his years living near San Diego.

Rancho del Descanso was opened to the public but drew little attention until the County Supervisors thought of selling and subdividing the land. Quickly, nearby residents formed the Descanso Gardens Guild, which saved Descanso as a public haven. Now the gardens are managed by members of the volunteer Guild.

In our quest for shade, we may come first to the Summer Circle Garden, just inside the entrance. This is often planted in bright colors, with annuals and eye-catching vegetables like the long Chinese gourds. Just beyond is a leafy refuge: an ancient live oak, covering the tram stop with a 100-foot circle of shade.

Walking west, you'll pass the famed Rosarium, with its rose collection out in bright sunshine. Look in from the shade of the beautiful native sycamores along the Rosarium's southern edge. Following your map, you'll reach the Bird Observation Station & Lake. If you're there early, it's a fine spot for birding.

Turning back to the east, you can wander at will through the oak and camellia forests. Green shade alternates with golden shade, and there are many benches. In the summer, dozens of spiders embroider their webs on the air. Casual paths meander here and there, and you can too, in and out of the woodsy sunshine.

How to get there: Descanso is at 1418 Descanso Drive. From the 210 Freeway, exit at the Angeles Crest Highway and drive south to Foothill Blvd. Turn right, and follow signs to the Gardens. Call (818) 952-4400.

Lanterman House
✧ *La Cañada Flintridge* ✧

WHICH IS MORE INTRIGUING, the family or the house, now
the only building in La Cañada Flintridge on the National Register
of Historic Places?

Development of the La Cañada Valley began when Jacob and
Amoretta Lanterman arrived from Michigan in 1875. With Colonel
A. W. Williams, they purchased some 5,800 acres and subdivided it
along a central axis road they called Michigan Avenue (today's Foothill Boulevard.)

Their land stretched from the Arroyo Seco to Tujunga. But water
was scarce in the little valley, and it was isolated from the town of
Los Angeles by the Verdugo Hills. Pasadena was just a village, sometimes inaccessible across the Arroyo stream. Eventually citrus, grapes,
and barley grew on the Lantermans' property.

Their son Roy, a physician, served in a relief hospital after San
Francisco's 1906 earthquake, then returned to build his own La
Cañada home in 1915. Today it is known as the Lanterman House.
Perhaps earthquake memories inspired its construction, which is
entirely of reinforced concrete. Rough granite for the chimney was
quarried near today's Descanso Gardens.

The next generation of Lantermans included Roy and Emily's sons Lloyd and Frank. The two brothers never married and lived together in the house until their deaths in 1981 and 1987. Lloyd was an inventor and tinkerer whose projects are in the house today. Frank was a State Assemblyman from 1950-78, and his life of politics and service is exhibited in the house.

When Lloyd left the home to the city of La Cañada Flintridge, it had been lived in by only one family. Furthermore, the two brothers had changed almost nothing since the house was built. Kitchen, bathrooms, porches had never been modernized.

You will see a household of 1915. The U-shaped home has 32 pairs of French doors to admit light and breezes. There is no central hall, but the downstairs rooms open onto the courtyard for air. The large living room and dining room hold the same furniture the original Lantermans put there: solid, prosperous, dark woods and Oriental rugs on the concrete floors.

Best of all, an artist is restoring the beautiful wall paintings that edge each room. These are not stencils but handpainted motifs of great variety. In the light-filled ballroom upstairs, painted roses and ribbons decorate Emily's space for entertaining. Below, Roy's billiard room is bordered in mannish browns.

The restoration methods are well illustrated for visitors. The house was much water-damaged when the city acquired it, and the artist had to trace nearly ruined designs, then painstakingly recreate the outlines for his careful brushwork.

Several exhibit areas also give insight into La Cañada's early history. Large photo murals show the surrounding valley in fascinating views.

How to get there: The house is at 4420 Encinas Drive. From the 210 Freeway, exit at Foothill Blvd. and drive west, angle left at Verdugo Road, then turn left on Encinas. Call (818) 790-1421.

St. Luke's of the Mountains Church
◇ *La Crescenta* ◇

LOVERS OF STONE ARCHITECTURE in the Southern California foothills: here's one for you. The little stone church in La Crescenta is St. Luke's of the Mountains.

A developer of this area in the early 1900's, M. V. Hartranft of Tujunga, told his fellow settlers: bring only a trowel and a sack of cement…there's plenty of sand and stones to build your home. And so there was, all along the mountain edges.

In the 1920's the houses in La Crescenta were week-end or temporary dwellings of people who had come for their health. One of these was S. Seymour Thomas, an artist born in Texas and trained in Europe as a portrait painter. In 1923 local citizens met at his home to plan an Episcopal Church for the valley. An acre of land on unpaved Foothill Boulevard had been donated by Mrs. Louisa Janvier.

That morning Mr. Thomas went

to the lot and quickly made a painting of his "dream church" for that spot: stone walls, a red tile roof, and the mountains behind. This became the design. (The little painting is on view today at the church.)

Later he walked among the field stones of the area and marked the ones for the building. These were retrieved by parishioners and the cornerstone was laid on Easter Sunday, 1924. The building's architect made for the occasion an inscribed copper trowel with an enamel picture of the church, given to the officiating bishop. After the ceremonies, all went for tea at the Thomases' nearby home, known as Cuddle Doon.

The original interior of the church, according to newspaper accounts, was a delicate greenish yellow, with pews stained green. Several stained glass windows were made by the famed Judson Studios, on the Arroyo Seco in Los Angeles. Later other colorful memorial windows were added.

A set of chimes was dedicated in 1926 as hundreds of people stood to listen on nearby roads. But one night the mechanism went awry and the chimes rang all through the night. "Chimes on Rampage" grumbled a brief newspaper note.

Scrapbooks in the church files trace activities of the parish and the surrounding times as well. The 1940s saw Red Cross work, and a notice to members during wartime rationing reads "Save some gas to come to the Christmas Tea!" In the 1950s a former stone fire house of the town (on Foothill Blvd.) was converted to the church's counselling center.

St. Luke's of the Mountains held quite an unusual event in 1992: a 100th wedding anniversary reception for Stephen Seymour Thomas and his bride Helen (who had died in 1956 and 1942 respectively). In this way the parish honored the health seeker whose quick oil sketch of a church had "come to life" just as he drew it.

How to get there: St. Luke's is at 2563 Foothill Blvd. From the 210 Freeway, exit at La Crescenta Ave. and drive north; turn right on Foothill. Call (818) 248-3639.

Sunland Park

✧ *Sunland* ✧

NO, YOU WILL NO LONGER FIND ferris wheels, "sky rides," and a miniature railroad at Sunland Park in the city of Sunland, but so it was in the 1940s. The wooded spot drew visitors even from neighboring counties, to enjoy the oak-shaded setting near the Verdugo Hills.

The Sunland-Tujunga valley was once in the rancho claimed by Jose Maria Verdugo. Later homesteaders came into the Tujunga Canyon, and 2300 acres of the valley land were bought by Judge Sherman Page and F.C. Howe in 1884.

They subdivided these holdings into one and ten acre tracts and named their town Monte Vista (now Sunland).

A depression followed the 1880s land boom, but some settlers were able to survive with orchards, vineyards, and bee-raising. Sunland Park was set aside in 1885 to be a community retreat, preserving a stand of ancient oaks.

From 1900 to 1906 the one-room Sunland School was in the park, with attendance ranging from 12 to 20 in the eight grades. In winter rains, the little building was sometimes surrounded by water and school cancelled for a while.

In its heyday, the park held thousands of people on summer days, for picnics, baseball, croquet, band concerts and sings. In the 1940s, a playland of eleven rides was the most fun for miles around. A Coney Island atmosphere prevailed: have a cotton candy, a ride on the miniature train, then a whirl into the sky on the fancy wheel.

Choose dancing indoors or out, or a dip in the giant oval swimming pool. Civic groups like the Kiwanis sponsored some of these larks.

Sunland is proud of its movie history, too. Filmed at Sunland Park were D.W. Griffith's first talkie ("Abraham Lincoln", 1924), Mary Pickford's first talking movie ("Coquette", 1929) and "It Happened One Night" with Clark Gable and Claudette Colbert in 1934. This one is still remembered locally as Sunland's finest. It was the first film to win all five of the major Oscars.

About that time the Sunland post office was serving 198 families. In those years, pre-World War II, life was still unhurried in the valley between the San Gabriel Mountains and the green Verdugo Hills.

By the early 1950s, Sunland-Tujunga was promoted as a highland valley "above the noise and turmoil of street cars, heavy traffic, and that cramped feeling of being fenced in." Eventually the two communities filled up the valley from hills to hills, but Sunland Park still remains as a peaceful retreat.

The original stone barbecues are there and baseball carries on in the recreational spot enjoyed for more than 100 years.

How to get there: Sunland Park is at Sunland Blvd. and Foothill Blvd. From the 210 Freeway, exit at Sunland Blvd. and drive east to Foothill. Contact the Sunland - Tujunga Historical Society at the Bolton Hall Museum: (818) 352-3420.

McGroarty Art Center
⬦ *Tujunga* ⬦

IN AN OAK-FRINGED NICHE of the Verdugo Hills is the house called Chupa Rosa. Warm days or rainfall bring native aromas from its twelve acres of chaparral. This is the former home of a distinguished Californian, now converted into the McGroarty Art Center.

Creative re-use of a historic building is always cause for celebration. The artistic hubbub going on in his house would probably delight John Steven McGroarty, poet, historian, playwright, and journalist, who built the home and lived there until his death (1923-44).

McGroarty was once widely known as author of the epic Mission Play, which was performed in San Gabriel at the Mission Playhouse. He was also chief editorial writer for the *Los Angeles Times* and wrote a column which ran for 40 years in that paper. Besides being California's Poet Laureate, he served in the U.S. Congress from 1934-38.

Locally, he helped to restore Olvera Street in Los Angeles and to reforest the San Gabriel Mountains. For years, his poem "Just Cali-

fornia" appeared in all history textbooks of our state. In 1932 the entire poem was worked in crochet by an admirer, and this curious tribute hangs upstairs in his home today.

The massive house is built of boulders and set into the bedrock of the hill. Thus anchored, it has not budged in recent earthquakes. The interior has hand-hewn beams and floor tiles made by Mexican craftsmen.

Upstairs, visitors may see the poet's library (his "glory corner"), with his books and memorabilia of his public life. Note a carved wooden chest, said to have been in Queen Isabella's Spanish palace. Literary mementos recall that he wrote 16 books of poetry and history.

Rancho Chupa Rosa was never a working ranch. The wooded slopes remained in a natural state and today they are a nature preserve.

After McGroarty's death, the house and twelve acres were purchased by the Los Angeles Department of Recreation and Parks in 1953 for $30,000. In 1970 the property was declared a Historic and Cultural Monument of the City.

Sometimes the drum and flute rhythms of Africa create a festive "village" of dance in the spacious living room. Another day a group of adults may work on oil paintings there, followed by children in piano classes. All this and more stirs up creative energy in the four studios of the house, now used as classrooms.

The City of Los Angeles provides upkeep for the building, while the Friends of the McGroarty Art Center volunteer hundreds of hours. Skilled artists offer classes in painting, drawing, ceramics, dance, quilting, stitchery, piano, storytelling, and more. Ages are 3 years through adults.

This is a comfortable spot, where imaginations are free to soar. Call for information on upcoming classes and events, or better yet, stop for a visit.

How to get there: The Center is at 7570 McGroarty Terrace in Tujunga. From the 210 Freeway, exit at Lowell; drive north to Foothill Blvd., left to Plainview, then left on Plainview which becomes McGroarty Terrace. Call: (818) 352-5285.

Bolton Hall Museum

✧ *Tujunga* ✧

THIS WAS THE Hope of the Little Lands: "…that there shall be the Life of the Open—the Open Sky and the Open Heart—fragrant with the breath of flowers, more fragrant with the Spirit of Fellowship…"

These ideals, on a hammered copper tablet in the Bolton Hall Museum, marked the 1913 founding of the Little Lands colony, about 200 hardy souls who settled in the area now called Tujunga. Their leader and inspiration was William E. Smythe, author and dreamer, who had already established agrarian communities in Idaho and San Ysidro, California.

Smythe had a Utopian vision of small plots, just an acre or two, where a family could support itself with crops, a goat and some chickens. He promoted the idea of irrigation through lectures and his magazine called *Irrigation Age*.

This is still a lovely valley between the Verdugo Hills and the San Gabriel Mountains. But the Big Tujunga Wash and Haines Canyon

have shed a difficult bounty over the years: hundreds and hundreds of rocks. As their crops struggled and World War I took some of their young men, the colony faded within a dozen years.

But not before the Little Landers had created a community meeting house that would outlast their dream. The saying goes, if life gives you lemons, make lemonade. Life had given the Little Landers rocks.

The clubhouse was built of those troublesome stones, in a solid rustic style with square tower and tile roof. Inside, a large all-purpose room has held town meetings, socials, church services, and a branch public library. The Chamber of Commerce and, briefly, the town jail were also here.

The designer of the Hall was George Harris, whose specialty was rustic architecture and "anything made in stone." Carved in the log mantel over the huge stone fireplace is his motto: "To the Spiritual Life of the Soil." Local historians have compared the fireplace to a natural cliff under which Indians might have built their fires.

Tujunga was annexed to the City of Los Angeles in 1932, and in 1962 the stone building was declared Los Angeles Historical Monument number two (following the Avila Adobe in Olvera Street).

However, recognition was one thing and survival was another. Bolton Hall, now surrounded by a growing but changing community, was closed and empty for nearly twenty years.

Vandals took their toll and demolition seemed near.

But with devoted efforts of the Sunland-Tujunga Little Landers Historical Society, the building reopened in 1980 as a museum and small research library. There you will find changing exhibitions of local history, plus information on spring house tours of the area. These usually provide a treasure hunt for other stone architecture of the early days.

How to get there: Bolton Hall Museum is at 10110 Commerce Ave. From the 210 Freeway, exit at Lowell Ave., drive north; turn left on Foothill Blvd. and right on Commerce Ave. Call (818) 352-3420.

About the Author

Elizabeth Pomeroy holds a Ph.D. in English from UCLA. She is an avid traveler and walker who teaches English at Pasadena City College. She has written literary studies and books on Queen Elizabeth I and John Muir, as well as articles about regional history. Her home is a restored Pasadena bungalow.

About the Artists

Joseph Stoddard is an artist who lives and works in Pasadena. He has produced many images for books, posters and magazines about the Southland and never goes anywhere without his sketch book and miniature paint box.

Hortensia Chu is a graphic designer and illustrator who also resides in Pasadena. She has designed many book covers and collaborated with Joseph on other Southern California publications.

Photograph Credits

Farnsworth Park: Altadena Historical Society
U.S. Army Balloon School: Arcadia Historical Society
Chinese Courtyard Garden: Pacific Asia Museum
La Casita del Arroyo: Pasadena Heritage
Pasadena Playhouse: Pasadena Heritage
Pasadena Civic Auditorium: Pasadena Heritage
Landmark Buildings of PCC: Pasadena City College
Lacy Park as Wilson Lake: Pasadena Historical Society
The Eagle Rock: Pasadena Historical Society
Covina City Park: Covina Valley Historical Society
El Monte Rurban Homesteads: El Monte Historical Museum
Bailey House: Whittier Historical Museum
Early Buildings of Occidental College: Occidental College
Tunnel at the Southwest Museum: Southwest Museum

Notes

Notes